access to history

ELIZABETH I: RELIGION and FOREIGN AFFAIRS

Second Edition

John Warren

Hodder & Stoughton

A MEMBER OF THE HODDER HEADLINE GROUP

Acknowledgements

The front cover illustration shows Elizabeth I attributed to George Gower, reproduced courtesy of the National Portrait Gallery, London.

The publishers would like to thank the following individuals, institutions and companies for permission to reproduce copyright illustrations in this book: © Sudeley Castle, Winchcombe, Gloucestershire, page 13.

Every effort has been made to trace and acknowledge ownership of copyright. The publishers will be glad to make suitable arrangements with any copyright holders whom it has not been possible to contact.

Orders: please contact Bookpoint Ltd, 130 Milton Park, Abingdon, Oxon OX14 4SB. Telephone: (44) 01235 827720. Fax: (44) 01235 400454. Lines are open from 9.00 – 6.00, Monday to Saturday, with a 24 hour message answering service. Email address: orders@bookpoint.co.uk

British Library Cataloguing in Publication Data
A catalogue record for this title is available from the British Library

ISBN 0 340 84689 5

First Published 2002
Impression number   10 9 8 7 6 5 4 3 2 1
Year   2008 2007 2006 2005 2004 2003 2002

Copyright © 2002 John Warren

Typeset by Fakenham Photosetting Limited.
Printed in Great Britain for Hodder & Stoughton Educational, a division of Hodder Headline Plc, 338 Euston Road, London NW1 3BH by Bath Press Ltd, England.

Contents

Preface

To the general reader

Although the *Access to History* series has been designed with the needs of students studying the subject at higher examination levels very much in mind, it also has a great deal to offer the general reader. The main body of the text (i.e. ignoring the 'Study Guides' at the ends of chapters) forms a readable and yet stimulating survey of a coherent topic as studied by historians. However, each author's aim has not merely been to provide a clear explanation of what happened in the past (to interest and inform): it has also been assumed that most readers wish to be stimulated into thinking further about the topic and to form opinions of their own about the significance of the events that are described and discussed (to be challenged). Thus, although no prior knowledge of the topic is expected on the reader's part, she or he is treated as an intelligent and thinking person throughout. The author tends to share ideas and possibilities with the reader, rather than passing on numbers of so-called 'historical truths'.

To the student reader

Although advantage has been taken of the publication of a second edition to ensure the results of recent research are reflected in the text, the main alteration from the first edition is the inclusion of new features, and the modification of existing ones, aimed at assisting you in your study of the topic at AS level, A level and Higher. Two features are designed to assist you during your first reading of a chapter. The *Points to Consider* section following each chapter title is intended to focus your attention on the main theme(s) of the chapter, and the issues box following most section headings alerts you to the question or questions to be dealt with in the section. The *Working on . . .* section at the end of each chapter suggests ways of gaining maximum benefit from the chapter.

There are many ways in which the series can be used by students studying History at a higher level. It will, therefore, be worthwhile thinking about your own study strategy before you start your work on this book. Obviously, your strategy will vary depending on the aim you have in mind, and the time for study that is available to you.

If, for example, you want to acquire a general overview of the topic in the shortest possible time, the following approach will probably be the most effective:

1. Read chapter 1. As you do so, keep in mind the issues raised in the *Points to Consider* section.
2. Read the *Points to Consider* section at the beginning of chapter 2 and decide whether it is necessary for you to read this chapter.
3. If it is, read the chapter, stopping at each heading or sub-heading to note down the main points that have been made. Often, the best way of doing this is to answer the question(s) posed in the Key Issues boxes.
4. Repeat stage 2 (and stage 3 where appropriate) for all the other chapters.

If, however, your aim is to gain a thorough grasp of the topic, taking however much time is necessary to do so, you may benefit from carrying out the same procedure with each chapter, as follows:

1. Try to read the chapter in one sitting. As you do this, bear in mind any advice given in the *Points to Consider* section.
2. Study the flow diagram at the end of the chapter, ensuring that you understand the general 'shape' of what you have just read.
3. Read the *Working on ...* section and decide what further work you need to do on the chapter. In particularly important sections of the book, this is likely to involve reading the chapter a second time and stopping at each heading and sub-heading to think about (and probably to write a summary of) what you have just read.
4. Attempt the *Source-based questions* section. It will sometimes be sufficient to think through your answers, but additional understanding will often be gained by forcing yourself to write them down.

When you have finished the main chapters of the book, study the 'Further Reading' section and decide what additional reading (if any) you will do on the topic.

This book has been designed to help make your studies both enjoyable and successful. If you can think of ways in which this could have been done more effectively, please contact us. In the meantime, we hope that you will gain greatly from your study of History.

Keith Randell & Robert Pearce

Introduction: Elizabeth I: Religion and Foreign Affairs

POINTS TO CONSIDER

This brief chapter is intended to introduce the main issues in religion and foreign affairs in the reign of Elizabeth I and to provide some insight into the context which gave those issues shape and importance.

KEY DATES

1533 Elizabeth born.
1536 Execution of Anne Boleyn.
1547 Death of Henry VIII.
1553 Death of Edward VI, accession of Mary I.
1558 English lose Calais. Death of Mary I, accession of Elizabeth I.
1603 Death of Elizabeth I.

1 A Remarkable Woman

In 1603, in the forty-fifth year of her reign, Queen Elizabeth I was clearly dying. Her secretary of state, Sir Robert Cecil, approached where she sat and told her that she should go to bed. Elizabeth rounded on him, saying 'Little man, little man! The word "must" is not to be used to princes'. In her rebuke is a theme central to this book: the Queen's sense of the high majesty of her position and title. But her sharp and dismissive words are as clearly the words of a remarkable woman. And one of the most remarkable aspects of her long reign was her ability to break most of the rules. These rules were made by men. The first and most important was based on the idea that a throne held by a woman was at best a misfortune. It was, therefore, the rule that a queen be taken under an appropriate male wing through a suitable and swift marriage. But Elizabeth I chose not to marry, and so did not, despite all the considerable pressure her (male) councillors and her (male) parliament could apply. She might at least be expected to name a successor, but she would not. A second rule was that no woman should have authority over the teaching of the Church. But the Church of England was, it will be argued, shaped very largely by the wishes of the Queen. A third rule was that a queen should pay heed to and follow the advice offered by her Privy Council – that select band (of men) who expected to hold the reins of government. And Elizabeth heeded that advice – sometimes, and when it suited her. If it did not suit, then the Privy Council was subjected to a formidable display of evasion, bullying and hesitation. She was also rather good at throwing slippers. Her secretary, Walsingham, caught one full in the face. Very occasionally, the Queen might be manipulated to take a course of action of which she disapproved. But it was not that her councillors succeeded in wresting control from her. The decision was hers.

Up to the very last years of her reign, Elizabeth I managed to baffle, irritate, drive to distraction but earn the admiration of this male-dominated world. Indeed, her reign fostered a public image which exploited the weaknesses of her position as a woman by converting them into strengths. Unmarried, she was represented as married to her country. Her successes – apparently so different from the supposed failures of other female rulers – were seen as evidence of God's favour. The childless Queen was presented in poetry, song and pageant as a kind of Virgin Mary, earning the undying love of her chivalrous countrymen. To the poet Spenser, she was the 'Faerie Queene', she was Gloriana: the untouchable and untouched. Her prestige was attested to by her enemies. Pope Sixtus V commented on how well she ran her country, despite her sex. 'She is only a woman, only the mistress of half an island, and yet she makes herself feared by Spain, by France, by the Empire, by all!'

2 Religion: Some Basic Assumptions

> **KEY ISSUE** Why was the relationship between monarch and Church so important?

It is not difficult to justify writing a book on the sixteenth century in which religious policy is a major theme. Religion, after all, played an enormous part in the daily lives of everyone. Life on earth was said by the Church to be nothing more than a preparation for what came after death: an eternity in heaven or an eternity in hell. Few, if any, doubted this. And few doubted that the Church was responsible for assisting its flock to do the will of God and, if possible, to achieve salvation. How much it influenced personal conduct day to day would vary from individual to individual. But every citizen was born into the Church through baptism, would be married by it, would attend its services on Sundays and receive its consolations before death. The Church had the right to pronounce on legal matters which involved some of the most important relationships between people, including social conduct and bequests through wills. Such services had, of course, to be paid for. Small wonder, then, that the Church was a major landowner and its bishops men of considerable secular power. Apart from income from the gifts of land, money and property bestowed through the ages, the Church received tithes – an annual payment based on a tenth of a person's income (from certain types of agricultural produce).

To understand the relationship between monarch and Church requires a long perspective. That relationship was, throughout the Middle Ages, intimate but frequently strained. It had to be intimate because it was assumed that civil order and religion went together. Religion was a vital agent of control in a violent and disordered society, and one which no monarch could place in jeopardy. In theory, the task of the monarch was to protect the Church and Christian society. This did not, however, give a king any power to act as if he had spiritual authority over the Church. The king was not a priest since he was not ordained by the Church and therefore had no right to tell the clergy what to teach, to forgive sins or to perform any spiritual function. The ultimate source of doctrinal authority was the Pope, whose task it was to supervise the teaching of the Church and to appoint the important church officials throughout Europe. There is little doubt that the medieval kings of England resented clerical independence: hence the strain in the relationship.

3 The Henrician Legacy

> **KEY ISSUE** What impact did the reign of Henry VIII have on the English church and its relations with the monarchy?

It is essential to understand the impact of the reign of Henry VIII on the relationship between monarch and church. This is partly because it serves to illustrate how the tensions between Church and state and between monarchy and papacy erupted in a religious reformation which severed England from the Roman Catholic Church. Without an awareness of the Henrician legacy, it is impossible to understand either the personal religion of Elizabeth herself or the religious position of the country at her accession in 1558. Keith Randell's volume *Henry VIII and the Reformation in England* in this series provides full details of the issues surrounding the King's break with Rome. For our present purposes, it is sufficient to point out that the English Church was forcibly split from the Roman Catholic Church as a result of the Pope's failure to give Henry VIII what he most wanted: a divorce from his first wife, Catherine of Aragon. The demand for the divorce was largely for political and dynastic reasons. Henry's long marriage with Catherine had produced only one surviving child, Mary. To secure his dynasty, Henry needed a son. But marriage, in the eyes of the Church, was not instituted by God to be dissolved whenever an important person found it convenient. This is why decisions on divorce had to be made by the Pope – as head of the Church – and for reasons which might plausibly be seen as religious. Although Pope Clement VII might well have wished to comply with Henry in this matter, he was not in a political position so to do. The reasons need not detain us, but the Pope's delays and prevarications proved intolerable to Henry – especially when his future queen, Anne Boleyn, became pregnant by the end of December 1532. The child was Elizabeth – the subject, of course, of this book.

Henry's divorce (or, more strictly, annulment) was performed by Thomas Cranmer, his Archbishop of Canterbury, in defiance of the traditional authority of the Pope. The break with Rome was, there-fore, set in motion by largely political factors, but it provided the King with the opportunity to achieve that ascendancy over the Church of England which his predecessors may have coveted but never gained. As Supreme Head of the Church of England, he saw fit to intervene in doctrinal matters when it suited him. And, as Supreme Head, he had the chance to make money out of the Church on a scale his pred-ecessors could scarcely have contemplated.

The English Reformation itself cannot, however, be explained purely by outlining the political and dynastic motives of Henry VIII. Had the King not made his break with Rome, he would still have faced – in common with his fellow European monarchs – the move-ment nicknamed Protestantism. As an evangelical (gospel-based) the-ology based on the ideas of Martin Luther, Protestantism sought to replace what it saw as the self-seeking and man-made traditions and superstitions of the Roman Catholic Church with a religion derived, it was claimed, from the New Testament and the words of Christ that it contained. Lutheran ideas were by no means unknown in England before the break with Rome. It is possible that, allied to lay anticleri-calism (dislike of the power and functions of the priesthood), these ideas may have been a potent weapon for reformation with or without the King. But there is no consensus among historians as to how wide-spread anticlericalism or evangelicalism were. Very often, the reli-gious affiliation of the historian is reflected in his or her stance on the issue. Catholic historians like Christopher Harper-Bill[1] and J.J. Scarisbrick[2] present a picture of a generally popular Catholic Church. Scarisbrick, for example, sees the Reformation as a fundamentally political event whose religious implications were not realised by com-mitted Catholics until it was too late. The Anglican A.G. Dickens,[3] on the other hand, stresses the extent of dissatisfaction with the Catholic Church and points to a younger generation of educated laity whose evangelicalism provided the 'real dynamic' of the Reformation.

The evidence on anticlericalism and the spread of Protestant ideas is scanty and enables both sides of the debate to make a plausible case. There is little doubt, however, that men such as Cranmer and Thomas Cromwell – the King's chief minister – were influenced in differing degrees by Lutheranism. Evangelical ideas were also of interest to the circle around Queen Anne Boleyn. Although Henry himself disliked new ideas in doctrine, this Protestantism gained sufficient currency for influential factions to develop at various times at Henry's court. Although the last years of Henry's reign saw a reaction against vaguely Protestant ideas which had found their way into the doctrine of the Church of England, two of Henry's three children – his son, Edward (later Edward VI) and Elizabeth herself – were brought up in an atmosphere heavily tinged with Protestantism. At Henry's death in 1547, his son was still a minor. Effective power fell into the hands of the Lord Protector Somerset who, together with his rival and successor the Duke of Northumberland, had, by 1552, turned England into a country whose official religion was clearly Protestant. This does not mean that England was suddenly and enthusiastically Protestant. Rural England – remote from the influence of ideas spreading in London and in the major cities and ports – was more likely to be confused than enlightened in the short term by the increasingly dramatic changes. When Edward died in 1553, it was more important for the influential in the land to see legitimate inheritance prevail rather than Protestantism as such. An attempt by Northumberland to supplant Henry VIII's eldest surviving child and heir Mary was a disastrous failure. The staunch Catholic Mary I duly returned England to Catholicism.

4 The Legacy of Mary I

> **KEY ISSUE** Why is it a mistake to see England at the time of Elizabeth's accession as a Protestant country?

Historians used to speak of a 'reimposition' of Catholicism by Mary. This is inaccurate on two grounds. Firstly, it implies that a basically Protestant country was unwillingly under the yoke of a rejected religion. But, as has been suggested, committed Protestants were by no means a majority. Secondly, Marian reform could not be a simple reimposition of old-style Catholicism because it was politically impossible for her to claw back the former monastic lands from their powerful purchasers. Nor did the cult of saints, shrines and pilgrimages revive. However, treatment of unrepentant Protestants was harsh. At least 287 people were burnt for their beliefs. These included some of the best known Protestants such as the former Archbishop of Canterbury, Thomas Cranmer, and bishops such as Latimer and Ridley. The genuine heroism of their deaths gave English Protestantism its martyrs, and martyrs, as always, fanned support. But all this made the position of the Princess Elizabeth distinctly dangerous. She was widely seen as sympathetic to Protestantism, and could all too easily be made the unwilling focus of a plot against Mary. She survived such dangers narrowly, gaining much political astuteness in the process and remaining heir to an ailing queen.

When Mary died on 17 November 1558, Elizabeth's succession was undisputed. But she was not, it must be remembered, inheriting a relieved and Protestant kingdom. Instead, she faced an entirely Catholic religious hierarchy with great power both inside and outside Parliament. Most influential Protestant clergy had been in exile abroad during Mary's reign, and knew more about the goings-on in the Protestant centres of Geneva, Frankfurt and Zurich than they did of the situation in their native country. At parish level, there was probably some confusion and apprehension engendered by 20 years of changes and uncertainty. In some areas of the country remote from London, Protestantism had made no impact whatsoever. When the City of London welcomed the new queen as a Protestant saviour by presenting her with an English bible and treating her to a display which showed Truth trampling Catholic Superstition, this was the wishful thinking of a minority and not a token of her country's views. The shutters had not come down on Catholicism with the death of Mary I.

5 Historians, Elizabeth and Religion

> **KEY ISSUE** What are the main areas of historical debate on Elizabethan religion?

One of the delights of studying Elizabethan religion is that there is no orthodox interpretation of it. The debate over the relative strength of Catholicism and Protestantism in the reigns of the earlier and mid-Tudors continues into the reign of Elizabeth I. We have already made the acquaintance of A.G. Dickens, whose masterly *The English Reformation* was first published in 1964. In stressing the considerable impact of Protestantism before the time of Elizabeth, Dickens necessarily argued that, by the time of the Queen's accession, 'the majority of people cannot possibly have been ardent or even convinced Catholics'.[4] Dickens also added that the bench of Marian bishops inherited by Elizabeth in 1558 was 'depleted' and by no means spoiling for a fight to defend its religion. Catholicism, therefore, was something of a spent force. Dickens deals with Elizabeth's relations with Catholics in a mere two pages as part of a chapter significantly entitled 'The Residual Problems'. However, Dickens's interpretation has been very effectively attacked by self-consciously 'revisionist' historians who have accused him of overplaying the appeal of Protestantism. Christopher Haigh, for example, has argued that no 'rapid reformation' took place.[5] There was no Protestant walkover even by the middle years of Elizabeth's reign. In many regions, Protestant religious legislation had had little effect and faced serious opposition. Dickens is also accused of underestimating the positive achievements of Mary I's religious policies, although they were cut short by her premature death. Indeed, it is claimed that Dickens is guilty of assuming that Protestantism is to be equated with progress and liberty and that its triumph was inevitable.

However, in 1989, Dickens took the opportunity afforded by a second edition of *The English Reformation* to reply to his critics. In re-examining the primary evidence and taking into account latest research, he concludes that the revisionists are mistaken in their view that Protestantism before Elizabeth was the creed of a small minority only. A minority certainly, but a substantial one. Enthusiastic Catholics were also, he claims, in a minority. Many people were the victims of religious indifference created by years of confusion. What these people wanted was stability and that, he feels, was what Elizabeth I gave them. Significantly, Dickens admits that this issue of the relative strength of Catholicism and Protestantism is unlikely ever to be finally settled.

Historical debate also centres around the so-called Elizabethan religious settlement of 1559. The term refers to the legislation which laid down authoritatively and in detail the way the Church was to be run and also the conduct of services for every parish church in the country. Historians are interested in why the settlement took the form it did and what challenges it faced through Elizabeth's reign. Here, of course, the debate on Protestantism and Catholicism resurfaces. How much of a threat, for example, was Catholicism? This issue will be discussed in Chapter 4. Challenge to the settlement, however, also came from a Protestant direction. Those who came to be nicknamed 'Puritans' were dissatisfied with a Church of England they saw as all too reminiscent of the abominable Church of Rome – at least in structure, ritual and the dress of its ministers. Historians of the 'whiggish' persuasion have identified Puritans with the alleged growth in parliamentary power which they trace from opposition to the religious settlement in Elizabeth's reign through to the breakdown in relations between the monarchy and the House of Commons at the time of the English Civil War. Sir John Neale, for example, argued that a 'Puritan Choir' – or nucleus of committed Puritans in the House of Commons – pushed the Queen further than she intended to go in the 1559 settlement. The 'Choir' then agitated for further reforms which would have destroyed the existing church hierarchy based on bishops and replaced it with a more 'democratic' system known as Presbyterianism, where the laity had a greater say in the Church itself. This thesis has been subjected to bruising challenge by historians such as Norman Jones[6]: their arguments are discussed in Chapters 2 and 3.

Those readers who like straightforward facts and single interpretations will, no doubt, have been put off by this section of the chapter. But it is always best for historians and students to admit when the evidence does not permit firm conclusions. This is particularly true of the debate on Elizabethan religion – especially where evidence for the beliefs of ordinary people is cited to support an interpretation. Much of this evidence is difficult to quantify and, since it reflects local conditions, may or may not be symptomatic of the country at large. There exists no full-scale survey which effectively draws together ongoing research into local conditions. Although the author of this book accepts much of the revisionist criticism of Dickens's interpretation, it must be acknowledged that we lack, for example, a full statement of the revisionist case of the same quality and persuasiveness of Dickens's work. Perhaps the final words should be left with the author of *The English Reformation* himself. Dickens says of the Reformation:[7] 'The subject is seldom easy to handle and whichever side one supports one should remain conscious that the other side can also offer a formidable case!'[7]

6 Foreign Policy: An Introduction

> **KEY ISSUE** What effect might the Reformation have on the traditional assumptions about foreign policy?

Foreign policy and religious policy are inextricably linked. A Europe in turmoil through dynastic confrontation or the struggle between kings and nobles was a commonplace of the Middle Ages, but the Reformation challenged old assumptions and opened the prospect of a re-drawing of alliances. It also provided old adversaries with a new weapon to use if a state were to suffer internal religious conflict. Alternatively, it might encourage co-operation across national boundaries in the interests of Protestant or Catholic solidarity. In Elizabeth's reign, for example, there existed a group of influential councillors who argued that England faced an increasingly dangerous Catholic League in which France and Spain sought to rise above their habitual rivalries with the intention of destroying Protestant England.

This does not mean that all the old assumptions were discarded following the Reformation. In England throughout the sixteenth century, it was accepted that the making of foreign policy was the special preserve of the monarch. Not that a king or queen could suddenly declare an intention to invade, say, France without forethought, consultation with councillors or a convenient quarrel. But the final say rested with the monarch. This was a reflection of the assumption that the kingdom was his or her personal property. Foreign policy was, therefore, largely a means of protecting or adding to it. It was emphatically not a means of safeguarding the interests of subjects, although lip-service was, from time to time, paid to such considerations. It might be argued, of course, that the status of England as the most powerful Protestant nation in Europe forced monarchs to consider the spiritual needs of the people in making peace or war. Perhaps: but this was, as we shall see, a factor more likely to influence the activities of councillors than to disturb the self-interest of a king or queen.

7 The Foreign Policy of Henry VIII

KEY ISSUE What were the main characteristics of the foreign policies of Henry VIII, Edward VI and Mary I?

Since it would have been impossible for Elizabeth to start her reign with a clean slate, it is important to establish the nature of foreign policy as pursued by her immediate predecessors. As a young king of seventeen, her father Henry VIII sought military glory in the time-honoured manner: an attack on France. Indeed, his own list of titles included the French kingship. He might hope to make that claim a reality, but England could not challenge France on the bat-tlefield without assistance. Traditionally, England had looked to the Duchy of Burgundy as an ally against France. The duchy had become one of the many Habsburg possessions encircling France, but the Habsburg Holy Roman Emperor, Maximillian, and the ruler of Spain, Ferdinand, had priorities other than assisting Henry's grandiose schemes. Henry led expensive campaigns to France which resulted in little real achievement. France, in turn, had sought to invoke its alliance with Scotland. That northern king-dom was traditionally suspicious of England, and James IV attempted to exploit Henry's embroilment in France by invading the country in 1513. At Flodden Field, the Scots were massively defeated and their king was killed. Henry's sister Margaret – James IV's widow – was left as regent for her son. Indeed, Margaret's mar-riage into the Scottish royal line had enormous implications for the future. As we shall see in Chapter 6, Margaret's granddaughter, Mary Stuart, had a claim to the English throne from her Tudor grandmother which proved to be a major problem for Henry's own daughter, Elizabeth I.

Henry's manoeuvres with France and Scotland were reasonably traditional. However, the annulment of his marriage and the break with the Roman Catholic Church seemed likely to jeopardise his relationship with the Habsburgs. The Habsburg Charles V had inherited the kingdom of Spain and the lands of the Austrian branch of the family: he was also elected Holy Roman Emperor. But Charles was nephew of Catherine of Aragon, and no friend to enemies of the Catholic Church. This raised the prospect of a worrying alliance against England by the Catholic powers of Spain and France. The possibility of a Catholic crusade was a nightmare recurring at various stages in the reigns of Henry and his daughter Elizabeth. It disturbed the sleep of zealous Protestants in the Councils of the two monarchs. But others rightly pointed to the constant rivalry between the Habsburgs and the Valois of France, and slept more easily for this recognition of the political realities.

To the end of his life, Henry remained obsessed with the possibilities of glory, booty and land to be won at the expense of France, and was astute enough to realise that Charles V would seek an alliance with the English King against the Valois whatever religious differences or family pride dictated. By 1543, the Emperor and the King of England had agreed to a joint invasion of France, aimed at Paris. In fact, the allies pursued their own objectives once the main invasion was launched in 1544. Henry's campaign was ruinously expensive, and his obsession with France prevented him from exploiting military victories against Scotland and the death of James V by assimilating that country into his own realm. Futile attempts to secure the custody of James's baby daughter Mary for a future marriage to Henry's son Edward were nothing more than an attempt to deal with Scotland on the cheap. By the end of his reign, the country was notionally at peace with France, but nothing had been settled and the peace was unlikely to last.

8 Edward VI and Mary I

Edward VI was nine years old at the death of his father. Government rested in the hands of Lord Protector Somerset. Like Henry VIII, Somerset hoped to secure for the Tudor dynasty the crown of Scotland through the marriage of Mary Stuart and Edward VI: unlike Henry, he was prepared to go to considerable expense to pacify Scotland. His policy of installing permanent military garrisons there was costly and by no means effective. It merely stimulated the French to send in 10,000 troops to defend an ally they could not afford to lose. For good measure, the French occupied Edinburgh and took Mary Stuart to France for marriage to the heir to the French throne. Somerset's fall was undoubtedly precipitated by the disasters of his Scottish policy. His successor, Northumberland, repaired the damage as best he could by seeking and achieving peace with France – at the cost of abandoning Boulogne: the one tangible prize of Henry VIII's final campaigns.

The foreign policy of Mary I used to be treated by historians as a disaster. It is true that Mary's decision to marry the Habsburg King of Spain, Philip II, aroused fears that England would be used to serve Spanish needs in their perennial conflict with France. When England joined in the war against France in 1557, such fears appeared to be justified. In January 1558, the sole remaining possession of the

English Crown on French soil – Calais – was captured by French forces. However, it is now generally accepted by historians that Mary did not unthinkingly yoke a protesting England to Spanish foreign policy. The Queen's Council agreed to declare war on France only after an attack on Scarborough by French-based English Protestants. But what matters most is the contemporary reaction to the loss of Calais. That is easily stated: it was one of bitter humiliation. Peace negotiations started in May 1558, but Mary died before they were complete.

Mary's marriage with Philip had failed to produce the child she so ardently desired: a child to secure a Catholic succession and to compensate the ageing Queen for the many sorrows of her life. The throne was Elizabeth's: no Catholic, as Mary knew all too well. So, it was a new queen whose representatives engaged in the peace process at Cateau-Cambrésis in the knowledge that England was in a vulnerable position. The country was still officially at war with a France whose troops were in Scotland and from where Mary Stuart was claiming the English throne as the legitimate Catholic heir.

9 Historians and Elizabethan Foreign Policy

> **KEY ISSUE** What are the main areas of debate on Elizabethan foreign policy?

Historians recognise that Elizabeth and her councillors had to deal with some alarming problems in foreign affairs: problems exacerbated by religion. In Ireland, for example, the limited authority of the English monarch was potentially threatened by that country's stubborn Catholicism. It was possible that foreign antagonists might seek to exploit this by encouraging rebellion. This issue is discussed fully in Chapter 6. Also in Chapter 6 is an assessment of English policy in Scotland: a country where the establishment of a Protestant regime in the early years of Elizabeth's reign was helpful from the English angle – providing that regime survived.

It was, however, the problems in continental Europe which most exercised Elizabeth and her councillors and which continue to exercise today's historians. As religious conflict afflicted first France and then the Netherlands provinces – the latter being under the control of the Habsburg Philip II – England could not remain indifferent. This was partly because neither France nor Spain would let her do so. If English Protestants could claim the existence of a Europe-wide Catholic conspiracy, then French or Spanish Catholics could similarly claim that England was behind a Europe-wide Protestant conspiracy. And the Netherlands offered good harbours for any Catholic power wishing to invade England to stamp out the alleged conspiracy. Moreover, the Netherlands markets were vital for England's economy.

Historical debate centres around the role of Elizabeth. In particular, historians argue over whether Elizabeth had firm foreign policy aims and, if so, how successfully they were achieved. R.B. Wernham,[8] for example, thinks that Elizabeth's Netherlands policy was characterised by consistent and defined aims which were successfully pursued. He identifies the aims as being based upon a fear of French influence over the provinces: Elizabeth's target was that they should remain Spanish but with some independence of action. However, Christopher Wilson[9] is much more dismissive. He concludes that Elizabeth's fear of France was real but mistaken, and that her behaviour over the Netherlands was characterised by indecision, panicky responses to events and eventual failure. A more even-handed interpretation is offered by Professor MacCaffrey.[10] He identifies her consistent principle as being that of preventing French expansion into the Netherlands, but concludes that she was essentially realistic in recognising her inability – due to lack of resources – to dictate events. Frequently, then, her approach was necessarily pragmatic. Of course, what is pragmatism to one historian is indecision and a regrettable failure to identify clear policy aims to another. However, historians who are tempted to criticise Elizabeth in this way perhaps overestimate the ability of a country with a comparatively small population to challenge larger and more powerful neighbours. Contemporaries certainly complained about Elizabeth's lack of ideals (by which they meant their own ideals), but modern historians need not follow them slavishly and rebuke the Queen for failing to be the Protestant champion of Europe or the creator of an independent Netherlands.

One of the most fascinating and instructive issues, and one which indeed illuminates the relationship between religion and foreign affairs, is that of the Queen and marriage. The prolonged and ultimately unproductive marriage negotiations with candidates of varying nationalities and chances of success give historians the opportunity to discuss Elizabeth's personality as well as the political and religious context in which decisions were made. Some interpretations, focusing as they do almost exclusively in the Queen herself, verge on 'psychobabble'. Others allow us to glimpse the complex interplay between religious belief, court intrigue, the Queen's own – and by no means consistent – wishes and the impact of events at home and abroad. Marriage and marriageability are discussed at length in Chapter 5.

Allegory of the Tudor Succession

References

1 C. Harper-Bill, *The Pre-Reformation Church in England 1400–1530* (London, 1989)
2 J.J. Scarisbrick, *The Reformation and the English People* (Oxford, 1984)
3 A.G. Dickens, *The English Reformation* (London, 1989)
4 ibid., p. 349.
5 C. Haigh (ed.), *The English Reformation Revised* (Cambridge, 1987)
6 N. Jones, *Faith by Statute: Parliament and the Settlement of Religion* (London, 1982)
7 Dickens, op.cit., p. 381.
8 R.B. Wernham, *The Making of Elizabethan Foreign Policy* (Berkeley, 1980)
9 C. Wilson, *Queen Elizabeth and the Revolt of the Netherlands* (London, 1970)
10 W.T. MacCaffrey, *Queen Elizabeth and the Making of Policy* (Princeton, 1981)

Working on Chapter I

This chapter does not require detailed note-making. It would be a good idea to work in pairs or groups to offer and therefore to compare your answers to the key questions. Any confusion or misunderstanding can be identified and resolved as groups present their responses to the whole class.

2 The Elizabethan Religious Settlement

POINTS TO CONSIDER

The Elizabethan religious settlement is a convenient phrase used by historians to describe the organisation, ritual and teaching of the Church of England as enforced by Acts of Parliament, as amplified by the pronouncements of Archbishops of Canterbury and as defended rigorously by the Queen herself. In reading this chapter, you should bear in mind three questions. Firstly, what factors shaped the settlement of the early years of the reign? In particular, how far did it reflect the views of the Queen? The second question centres on Elizabeth's defence of the settlement. Why and how did she defend it? Finally, the chapter seeks to sum up Elizabeth's attitudes to the Church of England by examining its treatment at her hands. Did she act as a loving protectress, or as a harsh and exploitative guardian?

KEY DATES

1559 Acts of Supremacy and Uniformity.
Book of Common Prayer.
Injunctions and Visitations.
Act of Exchange.
1563 Thirty-nine Articles.
1566 Parker's *Advertisements* and the Vestiarian controversy.

1 The Religious Beliefs of Elizabeth I

> **KEY ISSUE** What factors predisposed Elizabeth towards
> Protestantism?

No complete understanding of the Elizabethan religious settlement is possible without an awareness of the personal beliefs of Elizabeth I. And no complete understanding of Elizabeth's religious beliefs is possible without an awareness of the impact of her extraordinary upbringing. It would, of course, be very convenient to have a clear statement of those beliefs – preferably from the Queen herself. But Elizabeth was not a convenient person, and no such statement exists. Her opinions were shrouded in the obscurity of some of her utterances, in her constitutional incapacity for making decisions and in the distortions of those who reported her views.

On her religious upbringing, at least, we can be relatively clear. That upbringing would certainly predispose her towards Protestantism. Firstly, we must not fail to take into account the circumstances of her birth. The Church of Rome was not alone in denying the legality of Anne Boleyn's marriage to Henry VIII. But, given the fact that the legitimacy of her mother's marriage went hand in hand with the break with Rome, it is not difficult to see that Elizabeth would associate her own right to the throne with opposition to the Papacy. Also, her education was distinctly Protestant. The Boleyn faction was very interested in Luther's views on church reform. A few days before her arrest, Anne Boleyn had entrusted her like-minded chaplain, Matthew Parker, with the spiritual welfare of her infant daughter. What use Parker was able to make of that trust is not clear, but Elizabeth's selection of Parker as her first Archbishop of Canterbury testifies at the very least to the strong attachment and loyalty Elizabeth felt towards her Boleyn ties and to the issues which the Boleyns held dear. The 'evangelical' (gospel-based) stance of the Boleyns was reinforced by Elizabeth's subsequent education when Queen Catherine Parr brought her back to court. Catherine was a convinced Protestant, and the education which Elizabeth and her half-brother Edward received reflected the Queen's convictions.

Any attempt to establish the precise nature of Elizabeth's Protestantism must be based upon inferences from her actions. As far as possible, these inferences will be made in sections three, four and five of this chapter, where these actions will be analysed. As suggested earlier, her reported words are less easy to assess. We have a number of ambassadors' letters which, on the face of it, appear to give precise information on her beliefs and intentions. Ambassadors, however, had a natural desire to present themselves to their monarchs as incisive, firm and effective. It is all too likely that the accuracy of their information suffered as much from this as from the Queen's undoubted mastery of the arts of evasion and ambiguity.

There is also a certain amount of anecdotal information. We have an account of the frosty reception given by the Queen to a New Year's gift from the Dean of St Paul's in 1561. The Dean, it seems, had left a prayer book by the Queen's place in the cathedral. The book contained elaborately engraved pictures of saints and martyrs.

1 Here a remarkable passage happened, as is recorded in a great man's memorials, who lived in those times. When she [the Queen] came to her place, she opened the book, and perused it, and saw the pictures; but frowned and blushed, and then shut it (of which several took
5 notice) ... After Sermon ... applying herself to the Dean, thus she spoke to him:

Q. Mr Dean, how came it to pass that a new Service-book was placed on my cushion?

To which the Dean answered:

10 D. May it please your Majesty, I caused it to be placed there.

Then said the Queen:

Q. Wherefore did you so?

D. To present your majesty with a New-year's gift.

    Q. You could never present me with a worse.
15 **D.** Why so, Madam?
    Q. You know that I have an adversion to idolatry, to images and pictures of this kind.
    D. Wherein is the idolatry, may it please your Majesty?
    Q. In the cuts resembling Angels and Saints: nay, grosser absurdities,
20   pictures resembling the Blessed Trinity.
    D. I meant no harm: nor did I think it would offend your majesty ...
You must needs be ignorant then. Have you forgot our Proclamation
against images, pictures, and Romish relics in the Churches?

The Queen clearly had a gift for telling people off. One imagines a
stammering, red-faced and apologetic cleric who was left in no doubt
as to the Queen's dislike for anything she considered too close to
Roman Catholicism. By 'Romish' she meant Roman Catholic, and by
both she meant superstition and the worship of false images in the
place of God. Indeed, it is significant that Elizabeth's personal religious
books – or, at least, those that have survived – are plain and
unadorned. In Protestant fashion, there are few images. And in one
book, *The Litany, with certain other devout and godly meditations*, there is
a final prayer to God as 'the only ruler of all princes'. To link royal
authority so closely to that of God was characteristic of Elizabeth I.

2 Supremacy and Uniformity: The First Moves

> **KEY ISSUES** What were the advantages and disadvantages of each
> of the Queen's possible decisions on a religious settlement? What
> signals did Elizabeth make of her religious intentions before the
> meeting of her first parliament?

It was vital for the new Queen to signal her religious intentions, not
only to relieve dangerous uncertainty amongst her own subjects, but
also to avoid turning the perilous international situation into a thorough-going
disaster. What were her options? First, she could maintain
the Catholicism of Mary Tudor. This would indeed have its advantages.
Signalling Catholicism would preserve the alliance with
Catholic Spain, whose help she desperately needed in the continuing
conflict with France and Scotland. On the other hand, as we have
seen, there is little doubt that Elizabeth's personal preference lay with
Protestantism. Her surest supporters were Protestant, and she could
not afford to abandon them. Also, failures in Marian propaganda and
policy had enabled Protestants to link the burnings of martyrs with
submission to Rome, and the policy of submission to Rome with subservience
to Spain. Her second option would be to maintain the kind
of Catholicism without the Pope which had seemed, at times, to suit
her father. It could be argued that, since Elizabeth was the living

symbol of Henry VIII's break with Rome, she would naturally feel an attraction for following in his footsteps. However, since those footsteps wavered and lurched theologically to suit their master's mood and political convenience, they would prove immensely difficult to pursue under the vastly different political and religious circumstances confronting Elizabeth.

The third option was for Elizabeth to signal a moderate form of Protestantism. To do this would indeed prove politically sound at home in the short term, but a strident, Genevan-style reform would be another matter. The adoption of the model of John Calvin's reformed Church of Geneva would result in a wholesale destruction of all aspects of Catholicism. This in turn would create immense problems. Firstly, it would presuppose the readiness of the country at large to accept the confusion of a further change of worship. Protestantism of the Calvinist type, with its emphasis on the sermon and the Word of God, arguably required a literacy and education many did not possess. It would also remove church rituals which were often valued by communities because they fitted into the cycle of the seasons and the working year. Blessings at sowing time might be condemned as superstitious by contemporary Protestants, but nonetheless gave a sense of reassurance to the traditionally minded villager for whom the failure of a crop might mean something worse than hunger. After all, the radical Protestant reforms of Edward VI's time had themselves aroused resentment, and, as a consequence, disturbed local harmony. Secondly, in destroying the medieval system of church government through bishops, it might deprive the Crown of the mechanism it used to maintain control over the Church. Thirdly, and of greatest immediate importance, this form of Protestantism would utterly alienate Philip II of Spain – Elizabeth's brother-in-law and potential suitor – to the extent of convincing him of the need to make common cause with the French against a woman who proclaimed her heresy from the rooftops.

Any sudden change of religious direction would also cause practical problems for the Queen. Quite simply, the authorisation for such a change could not be given by the monarch alone. The reigns of Elizabeth's father, brother and sister had provided a precedent which suggested that religious change should proceed by the action of the sovereign in Parliament. The monarch needed to secure the acceptance of both Houses of Parliament before any major change in religion could be enacted. While the Henrician Parliament was limited to enacting decisions made outside itself, religious change under Edward VI and Mary I had emphasised the role played by Parliament. In the words of the historian Robert Ashton: 'What Parliament had done, only Parliament could undo.'[1] So, before making changes in religion, Elizabeth would have to bear in mind the attitude of the Catholic Marian bishops in the Upper House. If she wished for their co-operation, no radical Protestant approach would be possible.

The signals Elizabeth *did* make reveal not only her adherence to a milder form of Protestantism but also a considerable political astuteness. Apart from that Protestantism, she seems to have kept two principles firmly in mind as she entered into the stormy waters of a religious settlement. The first was the need to establish a national Church which would seek to secure the religious conformity and attendance of as many of the Queen's subjects as possible. This desire to make the Church at least acceptable to the majority rested on the assumption that no stable government could exist where subjects accepted the political rule of a monarch but rejected her religion in large numbers. The second principle reflected the need to perform a tricky but sensible balancing-act to keep her likely (Protestant) supporters and her potential (Catholic) opponents reasonably happy until political circumstances made her less unwilling to tread on sensitive consciences at home and abroad. This is why the first signs made by Elizabeth to her subjects and to foreign powers were careful, cautious and anything but strident.

Norman Jones, in Christopher Haigh's *The Reign of Elizabeth I*,[2] reveals how the Queen sought advice on the treatment of the religious question. Richard Goodrich's advice, in his *Divers Points of Religious Contrary to the Church of Rome*, was simply that, until the time was right for the removal of the Marian bishops and for overt Protestant legislation through Parliament, the Queen might require the use of Henry VIII's English Liturgy (form of worship). This would preserve a basically Catholic Mass, but Goodrich also suggested that the priest should be instructed not to elevate the Host. In Catholic theology, the Host is the wafer (bread) which becomes in essence the body of Christ through the power of the priest. This transubstantiation – as theologians termed it – was denied by most Protestants. Since the raising of the Host was a sign that the bread had changed into Christ's body, to forbid the raising of the Host implied a rejection of transubstantiation.

It is therefore very significant that Elizabeth seems to have followed Goodrich's advice in forbidding the elevation of the Host at Mass in the Royal Chapel on Christmas Day, 1558. The officiating priest refused, and the Queen walked out. Similarly, in January 1559, she snubbed the monks of Mary's restored abbey of Westminster when they approached her with their ceremonial tapers (candles): 'Away with these torches,' she cried, 'We can see very well.' This was, after all, a very public snub, since it took place at the state opening of Parliament. The Protestants present would doubtless have been suitably encouraged, since monastic life had no place whatsoever in Protestant thought.

Elizabeth also took care to give the first opportunity to a noted Protestant to preach the officially sponsored sermon at Paul's Cross in London. One Catholic found himself imprisoned for his outspoken rejection of the sermon. On the other hand, we recall that Elizabeth told the Spanish ambassador that she intended simply to restore the form of religion as practised in the conservative final years of Henry VIII's reign: a form which many Catholics had found acceptable. Such skilful – and inconsistent – manoeuvrings kept Protestants reasonably happy, but did not deprive Catholics of hope for the future.

3 Supremacy and Uniformity – the Parliament of 1559

> **KEY ISSUES** What difficulties were overcome in passing the Bills of Supremacy and Uniformity? What were the main terms of the Acts of Supremacy and Uniformity?

As Parliament assembled in January 1559, the international situation remained uncertain. Elizabeth could take comfort from the fact that Spanish interests were very much bound up with her retaining the throne. This was because her foremost rival to the English throne, Mary Stuart, might otherwise unite in her person the monarchies of France, England and Scotland against Spain. Since Mary was Queen of Scotland, wife of the Dauphin (heir to the French throne) and the most obvious Catholic candidate for the throne of England, this possibility – however alarming to Spain and the Protestant party in England – could not be ruled out. In the short term, Elizabeth might take comfort from the genuine desire of all three countries to end the war, which had resulted in the loss of the English outpost of Calais at the end of Mary I's reign. But the negotiations taking place at Cateau-Cambrésis between France, Spain and England in February 1559 also presented an opportunity for Elizabeth to make an attempt – unsuccessful as it turned out – to gain much-needed prestige by securing the return of Calais.

It is difficult to identify precise links between these problems of foreign affairs and the immediate moves of Elizabeth's government towards a religious settlement. We might easily exaggerate the extent to which the delicate international climate dictated a cautious approach towards changes in religion. After all, Elizabeth showed herself more than prepared to try Spanish patience by raising the Calais question time and again in the negotiations at Cateau-Cambrésis.

In fact, the first three government bills presented to Parliament on the religious settlement were sufficiently radical to arouse determined opposition. One bill aimed to sever the connections with Rome re-established by Mary, and to endow the monarch with the title of Supreme Head of the Church of England, as last used by Edward VI. This was the Bill of Supremacy. The content of the other two bills, which aimed to establish a uniform pattern of worship, is not known for certain, but it seems likely that they included the re-adoption of the second – and unmistakably Protestant – prayer book of Edward's reign. Books of Common Prayer were not so much lists of prayers as a precise framework for the services in every church in the country. In other words, they made explicit, through ritual and through the wording and structure of services, the official doctrine of the Church. The Bills of Uniformity duly passed the House of Commons, but were rejected by the House of Lords. A second attempt was also wrecked by the Lords, who altered the bills beyond recognition and refused to repeal Mary's laws against heresy. The Marian bishops in the Lords maintained an unwavering opposition to both bills. The reasons behind this opposition are well explained in a speech to the House of Lords made by Bishop Scot of Chester in March 1559. Scot stated bluntly that Parliament had no right to meddle with matters of doctrine. How could laymen, he argued, have the audacity to pronounce on the teaching of the Church?

It had been expected that Parliament would be dissolved before Easter 1559. However, Elizabeth did *not* dissolve Parliament. The Peace of Cateau-Cambrésis, signed in April, had removed the French threat and eased the worrying situation in Scotland, where 10,000 French troops had been expected after Easter. With the spectre of invasion lifted, it may be that Elizabeth could afford to create some upset at home in pressing for a religious settlement more congenial to herself and her Protestant supporters. She had also learned that the Marian bishops were prepared to oppose any measure which tampered with Catholicism. It was therefore necessary to break the stranglehold of the Catholic bishops and nobility over the House of Lords. The government had considered arranging a disputation (debate) between Catholic and Protestant clergy even before the Lords had mangled the Bills of Supremacy and Uniformity. This disputation duly took place in Holy Week and was presided over by Lord Keeper Bacon. Aggressive propositions attacked the authority of the Pope, the spiritual value of the Mass and the use of Latin in public worship. Arguments between Bacon and the Catholics led to the withdrawal of the latter, and gave Elizabeth the opportunity to arrest two of the departing bishops on a charge of disobedience to her authority. This reduced Catholic numbers in the Lords, gave the government a greater chance to push through openly Protestant measures and showed the Catholic laity in the Upper House that the government was determined to override opposition.

After the Easter recess, Parliament was therefore presented with new Bills of Supremacy and Uniformity. The Queen did *not* claim her father's title of Supreme Head of the Church of England, in deference to the widely held view that a woman could not exercise spiritual authority over the Church. Instead, the title 'Supreme Governor' was substituted. This allowed her apologists such as John Aylmer – a Protestant exile during Mary's reign and a future Bishop of London – the opportunity to accept that, whilst the New Testament clearly excluded a woman from performing a spiritual ministry, there was nothing to prevent a woman from acting as a kind of overseer to the Church. Aylmer was, in fact, responding to the charge of his fellow Protestant John Knox that no woman had a right to hold any civil or religious power over men whatsoever. As we shall see, none of this theoretical limitation of her power had much effect on Elizabeth's own interpretation of her rights over the Church. It had even less effect on her actual behaviour towards the bishops, who were the –clergymen responsible for making pronouncements on matters of doctrine. She expected obedience, and not instruction, from them.

The Bill of Supremacy also demanded that the clergy and royal officials swear on oath that they accepted the Queen's title. In addition, it sought to repeal the Marian laws on heresy, and to set up a Commission for Ecclesiastical Causes (the High Commission), which would itself have the right to judge on orthodox doctrine. The Marian bishops failed to muster enough lay support to block the passage of the bill: only one layman voted against it in the Lords. The Uniformity Bill had a considerably rougher ride through the Lords. Only the inexplicable absence of the Abbot of Westminster and the entirely explicable absence of the two bishops languishing in the Tower enabled the bill to pass.

The new Act of Uniformity required the use of a Book of Common Prayer in all churches, and provided a system of punishment for those who failed to use it, or who publicly objected to it. This 1559 book was based on the two Edwardian prayer books, of 1549 and 1552. However, the Queen insisted on an important amendment to the 1552 book, which had included the so-called 'Black Rubric' – a set of instructions to the clergy. This rubric had declared that kneeling at Communion must not be taken to imply that Christ was corporeally (bodily) present in the bread and wine. The 1559 prayer book instructed the priest to say the words of *both* the 1549 and 1552 books when offering the bread and wine at Communion. This was a straight compromise. It was just possible for a Catholic to take the words to mean that Jesus was really present in the bread and wine, and a Protestant could dwell on those which implied that Communion was taken as a memorial and celebration only. Elizabeth also removed insulting references to the Pope which had appeared in the 1552 book. The Queen's amendments demonstrate her concern to avoid the conflict which might have arisen if an Act of Uniformity adopted the kind of rigid theology which left many of her subjects outside the Church. Since the Act included the obligation to attend church on Sundays and Holy Days under pain of a fine of one shilling for every absence, it was important to give potential opponents every opportunity to conform.

The Act also incorporated instructions on the ornaments of the Church, which included the garments worn by ministers. The ornaments question was covered by clause 13:

1   Provided always and be it enacted that such ornaments of the church
     and of the ministers thereof shall be retained and be in use as was in
     the Church of England by authority of Parliament in the second year of
     the reign of King Edward the Sixth until other order shall be therein
5   taken by authority of the Queen's Majesty, with the advice of her com-
     missioners ... and also that if there shall happen any contempt or irrev-
     erence to be used in the ceremonies or rites of the Church by the
     misusing of the orders appointed in this book, the Queen's Majesty
     may, by the like advice of the said commissioners ... ordain and publish
10   such further ceremonies or rites as may be most for the advancement
     of God's glory, the edifying of his Church, and the due reverence of
     Christ's holy mysteries and sacraments.

Parliament also transferred from the Papacy to the Crown the right to
claim the taxes known as First Fruit and Tenths from the clergy, since
the laity were not displeased to see the Crown's income raised providing they did not have to contribute more themselves. Similarly,
most laymen were pleased to contemplate the potential profit to be
had from the dissolution of the monasteries and chantries founded by
Mary I.

4 Historical Interpretations of the Factors Shaping the Settlement

> **KEY ISSUE** How convincing is the Neale thesis that the settlement
> of 1559 owed much to the pressure applied by the 'Puritan
> Choir'?

The religious settlement of 1559 has provoked a major debate among
historians. To assess the different interpretations, it is necessary to
pose two questions. Firstly, what are the values and assumptions of the
historian in question? His or her world-view is likely to affect the way
in which subject matter and evidence are selected and approached.
Secondly, what method does the historian use in evaluating evidence?
That method may well reflect the formal and informal academic
training undergone.

Had this book been written in the early 1960s, it might well have
followed the prevailing interpretation, which owed much to the
writings of Sir John Neale.[3] In looking at the Elizabethan religious settlement of 1559, Neale stressed the role of Parliament – or rather, the
House of Commons – and argued that the Queen had been forced by
a well-organised and influential nucleus of Puritans within the
Commons to move further in a Protestant direction than she had
originally intended. He also argued that the Puritan faction, which he
called 'The Puritan Choir', increasingly used the Commons to force
the Queen into further reform of a Church of England which they felt

was too close to the Church of Rome and too far from Calvin's Church in Geneva. This loyal but frustrated opposition also demanded the right to advise the Queen on foreign affairs and on the thorny question of her marriage. This led them to become increasingly jealous of the 'liberties' and 'privileges' which, they claimed, belonged to Parliament. In recent years, Neale's thesis has been subjected to extensive and effective attack. Neale has been accused of the kind of distortion of evidence which comes from allegedly identifying some form of 'progress' which happens to suit an historian's political standpoint. In this case, he identified an increase in the power of the House of Commons, and then read back through history to trace a line of development. This tendency to treat history as a series of 'Rises' – the Rise of Protestantism, the Rise of Parliament – has been labelled as the 'Whig' school of history, where the values of liberal democracy are imposed upon the past to create a sense of inevitable progress.

We now need to consider the impact on Neale of his own academic training. He was the pupil of A.F. Pollard, whose interests were in the field of biography and political history. These led Pollard to ignore the actual workings of a body like Parliament in favour of portraits of the members of the House of Commons. Neale also relied heavily on biographies of Members of Parliament to establish his thesis of opposition to the relatively conservative religious policy of the monarch. The problem with this approach is that biographical detail of MPs does not, of itself, explain how Parliament operated as an institution. The behaviour of MPs was subject to many constraints, including the fact that it was the right of the monarch to summon and dissolve Parliament more or less at will. This meant that the wishes of a king or queen were more likely to influence parliamentary behaviour than the particular upbringings or convictions of certain members of the House of Commons. Nor does Neale pay sufficient attention to the relationship between the House of Lords and the lower House. An examination of the way in which Parliament functioned reveals that the upper House had the greater prestige and therefore a very considerable influence over the workings of the House of Commons.

Chapter 3 discusses Neale's claim that the House of Commons fell under Puritan influence and came to support demands for radical changes to the Elizabethan Church of England. For the moment, we need to look at that part of the Neale thesis which applies to the 1559 settlement. Was the Queen pushed into a more radical settlement than she had intended by an organised and disciplined group of Puritans, full to the brim of the latest reformed ideas picked up from their experience as exiles on the Continent? Did that group effectively control the House of Commons? The answer to both questions is no. The work of Norman Jones has demonstrated that there was no effective Puritan faction in the 1559 Parliament. He has calculated that there were no more than 25 MPs who could be considered

Calvinist or radical Protestant out of the 400 members of the Commons. Indeed, there were only four exiles among this 25. Nor were these so-called Puritans effectively led or organised. The dismantling of this part of the Neale thesis has two implications. The first is that the settlement itself, with its compromises and carefully contrived vagueness, represents more or less the wishes of the Queen herself. It is hard to overstate the importance of this conclusion, which not only forms the basis of the argument for the rest of this chapter, but also explains the determined way in which the Queen defended 'her' settlement. The second implication is that the major opposition in 1559 to such wishes came from the Catholic bishops and nobles in the House of Lords.

5 The Settlement in Action

a) The Settlement and the Bishops

KEY ISSUE Why did the Queen demand a Church of England with a Catholic-style hierarchy of bishops and archbishops?

The Queen might be Supreme Governor of the Church of England, but who was to be responsible for the detailed organisation, administration and supervision of the Church and its clergy? There was never any doubt in Elizabeth's mind that the episcopate – the bishops – should retain that function. This section examines the reasons for this decision. It also discusses the way in which the Queen selected her bishops, and seeks to examine Elizabeth's treatment of her episcopate. This will, in turn, shed light on both the nature of the settlement and the attitude of the Queen towards the Church.

Episcopacy was not the only possible system of church government. The most obvious alternative was that associated with Calvin's Geneva, where bishops had been discarded. The Genevan Church, whatever Calvin's personal influence might be, was not hierarchical in the sense of an episcopal Church. The supervision of beliefs and standards of behaviour in Geneva was carried out by an organisation known as the Consistory, members of which included ministers (the word 'priest' should not be used) and men of considerable social standing known as lay elders. It was the Consistory, and the discipline it was able to impose, which gave Calvinism the cohesion it needed to develop from small and local beginnings into a major movement, spreading into many states. This pattern of organisation was precisely why the Queen would never consider such a system. How could she control a Church which was based upon decision-making by a number of people who were often remote from the centre of power? How was she to make her wishes known? How much easier it would be for her if she could use her bishops to control, not only her clergy, but also her subjects. After all, it was not just Calvin's Church which claimed the right to deal with social behaviour: this had been a familiar duty of the Church throughout the Middle Ages.

There were other advantages to the Queen in retaining bishops. Should it be advisable for reasons of foreign policy to minimise the differences between the Church of England and the continental Catholic Church, then the shared institution of episcopacy would help a great deal. Finally, we must not underestimate the importance that Elizabeth attached to tradition. After all, her father had never discarded bishops.

Granted that the Queen had decided to retain the episcopate, she had one immediate decision to make in 1559 – which bishops? The Queen's first step was to encourage the Marian bishops to remain in office. However, their almost unanimous refusal to take the oath accepting the Act of Supremacy made this impossible. They were duly deprived of their offices, and the Queen turned to clergy of a Protestant persuasion: men who had been exiles during Mary Tudor's reign. In all probability, the influence of the Queen's Secretary, William Cecil, lay behind their appointments. These former exiles included Grindal (made Bishop of London), Cox (Ely), Jewel (Salisbury), Sandys (Worcester) and Young (Archbishop of York).

The Queen's manoeuvres here are not easy to interpret. It might be argued that the attempt to retain Catholic bishops reveals that Elizabeth was more interested in presenting an image of religious continuity than in securing full-blown Protestantism. This view generally complements the argument in section three of this chapter: namely, that the Queen wished to emphasise as far as possible certain familiar and traditional elements to avoid confusion and disorder. On the other hand, there is no escaping the fact that the Elizabethan settlement as defined by the Acts of Supremacy and Uniformity was distinctively Protestant. It may be that the Queen was unrealistic in hoping that Catholic bishops could be persuaded to enforce a fundamentally Protestant settlement. She could hardly have expected them to be enthusiastic in spreading Protestantism, but was clearly prepared to forego this in favour of her own interpretation of her political needs. Perhaps we should argue that the Queen was hoping that the Marian episcopate would fall into the mould of many of the bishops of her father's time: careerist clergy whose experience as royal officials gave them an in-built sense of loyalty to the monarch's demands and a willingness to make unpalatable compromises.

If we are right in arguing that Elizabeth's ideal bishop was first and foremost a loyal administrator, then it is clear why Elizabeth turned to the exiles only as second choices. Their recent experiences were not as crown servants, but as refugees whose religious ideals had forced them out of the country of their birth. To put it simply, how was the Queen to know whether men of this stamp would prove easy to control? How ready would they be to take on the traditional role of the bishop in political affairs? Indeed, some of them were clearly reluctant to accept a bishopric. In Geneva, in Zurich and in Frankfurt, they had seen in operation congenial religious organisations which had discarded the fundamentally Catholic system of episcopacy. Most were strongly influenced by Calvinism, and would expect the theology of the Elizabethan Church to follow suit. And they would also anticipate further reform of the organisation and ritual of the Church, where the Genevan model could be adapted to the needs of England. The Acts of Supremacy and Uniformity would be seen as a start – but no more than a start – to the reform process. The problem was that Elizabeth regarded it as the conclusion.

It is clear, therefore, that difficulties lay ahead for the new bishops. The first such difficulty occurred before they took up their offices. Under the 1559 Act of Exchange, the Queen was given the right to exchange property of a vaguely spiritual nature which she had in her possession for temporal (non-spiritual) property in the possession of the Church. On the face of it, this sounds fair and sensible. What it meant in practice was that things of limited value – like certain rectories, church buildings, rights to tithe – were exchanged for castles and manors of considerable value. The net result was that the Church lost considerable wealth. Initially, the aim was to make money out of the deprivation of the Marian bishops. But such legislation could be used by the government to put pressure on bishops reluctant to bow to the Queen's demands. It is also important to note the attitude of some Protestant laymen to the bishops. Quite simply, they did not like them. Some of the Marian bishops had been truly energetic in seeking to burn the heart out of Protestantism, and men of Cecil's stamp did not forget. At the very least, they were not likely to be enthusiastic episcopalians. Bishops, they felt, were all too inclined to pride. To cut the wealth of bishops – particularly in terms of church lands – would be an excellent method of curtailing their power and influence.

The Act of Exchange also interfered with the way in which bishops could deal with their lands. A bishop gained income from renting out land just like any other landowner. However, the Act prevented him from renting out land on leases lasting more than 21 years (except to the Crown). This was partly an attempt to keep the value of church land high, because long leases failed to take account of rises in land value and inflation. This is not, however, the action of a concerned administration worried about the income of bishops. Instead, it saw church land as a useful supplement to the Queen's patronage. If the Queen did not care to use her own money or crown lands to reward her nobility and gentry, then the bishops might be persuaded to grant favourable leases to such laymen. It was therefore in her interest to make sure that clerical land remained attractive. There was considerable protest from the bishops-elect over both aspects of the Act of Exchange. This kind of squabbling at the very birth of the Elizabethan

Church was unseemly and embarrassing to the government, which backed away from demanding exchanges. But the bishops were certainly subjected to pressure to grant leases to the nobility on favourable terms. To refuse the demands of a powerful nobleman who had the backing of Elizabeth was no light matter. Few bishops cared to do so.

It would therefore seem reasonable to argue that Elizabeth envisaged her bishops less as generals leading armies of Protestant shock-troops and more as subservient civil servants whose task it was to promote uniformity on the model approved by her, and whose incomes might be tapped whenever the Queen felt it necessary. Many bishops found this an uncomfortable role at best. The following sections of this chapter provide further supporting evidence of this interpretation. Chapter 3 discusses the grave consequences when Archbishop Grindal rebelled against that role and dared to remind Elizabeth that God was not only the true master of her Church, but also of her soul.

b) The Injunctions of 1559

> **KEY ISSUES** What were the details of the injunctions? What factors shaped those details?

This chapter has argued that Elizabeth sought to establish a basically Protestant settlement of religion, which nevertheless emphasised elements of continuity with the Catholic past in the interests of the stability of the Crown. The Royal Injunctions of 1559 confirm this view. As a set of instructions aimed at establishing the detail of a pattern of worship (based on the framework of the Act of Uniformity), they inevitably attacked certain Catholic practices. But they did not destroy all links with tradition.

Under the Injunctions, the clergy were to observe and teach the Royal Supremacy, and to speak against the Pope's alleged usurpation of the right of the monarch to govern the Church. The processions associated with the Catholic Church were almost entirely banned. Monuments to 'fake' miracles were to be destroyed, although the Injunctions stopped short of forbidding images in churches. Pilgrimages were, however, explicitly forbidden. Recusants (those who refused to attend the services of the Church of England) were to be denounced to the Privy Council (the monarch's inner circle of advisers) or to local Justices of the Peace.

If a Protestant had been asked how England was to be made a truly Protestant country, he would have said, 'Preach the Word of God, preach it again and preach it some more'. However, the Injunctions placed very clear restrictions on such evangelising. No preaching was to take place without official permission, which meant that a licence had to be obtained from the authorities. This move meant that preaching would be restricted to those clergymen who held a Master of Arts degree. But these men were few and far between. Even in the university diocese of Oxford, considerably less than half the clergy held such a degree. So, the run-of-the-mill clergy were restricted to reading from books of prepared pastoral advice. They then had to try to get hold of their better-educated brethren to preach the legal minimum of sermons, which worked out at about 15 per year. This seemed pitiful to many Protestants: worse still, it was depriving the Church's flock of the very words which might stir the most hardened and superstitious to seek salvation and obey the righteous demands of God. Why, then, did the Queen impose such restrictions? Most probably, the answer is because she saw unlicensed and possibly unlearned preaching as disruptive of good religious and civil order. Firstly, soul-hungry preachers swarming into traditionalist Catholic areas would almost inevitably cause trouble and dissension. Such preachers rarely showed a great amount of tact. A violent verbal assault on a villager's faith – the faith his forefathers had accepted unquestioningly – was unlikely to result in anything other than strong (and possibly physical) opposition. Second, the Queen had the dislike common to all sixteenth-century monarchs of seeing the lower orders gathered *en masse*. People attending open-air sermons were also people who might be swayed to criticism of her government. Elizabeth expected and demanded loyalty, but never took it for granted. She felt that loyalty was not a natural characteristic of subjects. Third, Elizabeth's use of the bishops as the instruments of her personal authority over the Church would be jeopardised by widespread and unlicensed preaching. How could bishops control and supervise large numbers of preachers? How could they be sure that preachers were not departing from the orthodox (standard and official) teaching of the Church, and thus stimulating disunity?

The Injunctions required that each parish church obtain a copy of the Bible in English and, significantly, a work by Erasmus – his *Paraphrases of the Gospels*. The latter is significant because Erasmus was no Protestant. His interest in reform and in translating the Scriptures did not carry him out of the Catholic Church. The presence of a work by him in each church suggests once again the intention implicit within the Injunctions: namely, to minimise the distance being travelled from the traditional Catholic ways. Indeed, other Injunctions sought to promote continuity in worship and uniformity in practice. The congregation was to bow at the name of Jesus, and to kneel at prayer. The clergy were ordered to wear distinctive clerical dress. In particular, they were to wear the garments specified in 1552 in the reign of Elizabeth's brother, Edward VI. These garments included the surplice – a white linen gown. As we shall see, its retention provoked controversy, since many Protestants – particularly those with experience of the continental reformed churches – saw it as a remnant of

Catholicism and all too similar to the garments worn by a Catholic priest when celebrating Mass.

On the issue of clerical marriage, the standard Protestant argument was that, since the minister did not have any special power granted by God, there was little need to separate him from other men. Marriage was therefore not only permissible, but was also to be encouraged. It was a mark of Catholicism to demand celibacy as a sign of the special status of the priest. However, the Injunctions stopped well short of accepting the full Protestant position. Clergy could indeed marry, but only with the special permission of their bishop and two Justices of the Peace. This curious arrangement probably reflects the Queen's personal and conservative distaste for married clergy.

c) The Visitations and the Crucifix Controversy

> **KEY ISSUE** How do the visitations and the crucifix controversy illuminate the different aims of the Queen and bishops?

We must distinguish between the moderate tone of some of the Injunctions and the result of the visitations (or inspections) which were designed to enforce them. Since a number of visitors were aggressively Protestant, images, relics, altars and uniquely Catholic clerical clothing ('vestments') were simply destroyed. And, since visitors were also empowered to examine the beliefs of the clergy and to punish those who refused to subscribe to the Act of Supremacy, the Book of Common Prayer and the Injunctions themselves, some 400 clergy either resigned or were deprived of their positions between 1559 and 1564. At least half of the departing clergy were openly Catholic. Clearly, the bishops of the Grindal mould must have felt that the anticipated further reformation above and beyond the 1559 Acts was proceeding according to their wishes. But the Queen had other ideas. Most bishops were dismayed when Elizabeth, in 1559, demanded that each church should retain a crucifix – the cross with the crucified Christ – and that those crucifixes destroyed during the visitations should be restored. This brought bishops such as Jewel and Sandys to the point of resignation, since they were being told to reinstate what they saw as an unequivocally Catholic ornament. The crisis was averted only when the Queen – uncharacteristically, but sensibly – backed down. However, she insisted that the crucifix remain in the Chapel Royal – where it would be seen by foreign ambassadors, who were then at liberty to stress the similarities between their own Catholic worship and that of the Protestant English Queen.

6 Archbishop Parker and the Vestiarian Controversy

> **KEY ISSUES** What was the nature and impact of the Vestiarian Controversy? How does it illuminate Elizabeth's religious policy?

The issues underlying the dispute over the crucifix resurfaced in the so-called Vestiarian Controversy. In January 1565, the Queen wrote to Archbishop Parker to demand that he used his authority to ensure that the rites and practices of the clergy did not deviate from the settlement of 1559. The Queen's desire to defend that settlement is a testimony to the importance she attached to it as an expression of her own wishes.

Parker, we recall, was Anne Boleyn's former chaplain and a man who had remained in the country throughout Mary's reign. He could be relied upon to give full weight to the authority of the monarch, and was, no doubt, the obvious choice from Elizabeth's point of view as her Archbishop of Canterbury. He was quite prepared to impose uniformity on his clergy at the monarch's command. The Queen was particularly concerned over the widespread flouting of the need to wear vestments as specified in the Act of Uniformity. Several bishops had turned a blind eye to clergy who had refused to use the appropriate vestments, and Parker had no hesitation in calling them to order. This suited the stress he placed on authority. It may even be, as the historian Collinson suggests,[4] that he asked the Queen to place her verbal complaints in writing so as to strengthen his hand in the troubles he knew lay ahead. It is characteristic of Parker that he expected and requested back-up from the secular arm when engaged in struggles with disobedient clergy.

In consultation with Grindal and other clerics, Parker published his *Advertisements* of 1566, in which he attempted to make a clear statement of exactly what was expected of the clergy in terms of doctrine, administration of prayer and the sacraments and, of course, clerical dress. Parker was clearly prepared to follow the Queen in requiring services to have an outward appearance of continuity of the past. Clergy were reminded that communicants were to receive bread and wine kneeling. The time-honoured font was to be used for baptism, rather than the more aggressively Protestant basin. But when it came to vestments, Parker showed a willingness to compromise. He decided that, rather than try to impose the full vestments as required by the 1559 settlement, he would settle for imposing the surplice only in parish church services. Dignitaries in cathedral and collegiate churches were expected to wear more elaborate vestments in addition. For outside wear, clergy were to have distinctive garb appropriate to their rank. In particular, Parker insisted on the traditional-looking square cap: only on long journeys could this be replaced by a hat. In March 1566, a curious fashion parade was held at his palace of Lambeth. The audience were the clergy of London, and on view were the correct vestments and outdoor wear. Of the 110 clergy present, 37 refused to accept clothing they judged to be papistical. They were duly suspended from their offices.

What these ministers objected to was not only the similarity between these garments and those of the Catholic priest. They also disliked the fact that the clothing seemed to suggest that clergy were a separate caste, with particular powers. We can take the Puritan Crowley's pamphlet against the *Advertisements* as an example of the objections the radical Protestant would have towards the surplice. Crowley argued that such garments could not be considered as an unimportant matter because of their association with the papists. He cited various biblical passages to try to prove that the surplice was actually and specifically forbidden, and reminded his readers of St Paul's injunction that all things should be done with the correct teaching in mind. He went as far as complaining that, if the monarch were able to order such things, it gave the impression that religion was of little moment, since it was at the mercy of a ruler's whim. A response – possibly by Parker himself – denied that ministers themselves had the right to make up their own minds on what was or was not effective and proper teaching. The writer added that this would be the first step towards granting every subject the right to determine the Queen's laws.

We do need to consider on what grounds the Archbishop felt justified in imposing such regulations, since he knew as well as any radical Puritan that there was nothing in the Scriptures about apostles, disciples or anyone else for that matter wearing surplices and square hats. The argument employed was that it lay within the Queen's authority to impose a certain standard of dress for the sake of civil order. This was a familiar idea: laws already existed whose purpose was to prevent the wearing of inappropriate dress by persons of insufficient social status. The dress of the clergy was not, after all, an issue affecting the salvation of themselves or their flock. Here we see employed the idea of *adiaphora*, or 'things indifferent', which the monarch had the right to enforce. Helpfully, influential continental reformers such as Bullinger in Zurich were prepared to accept the concept of *adiaphora*, and even to warn zealous Puritans that they need not worry their consciences over the matter. But not all were ready to accept moderate advice. The Vestiarian Controversy may have been limited to the capital and the universities, but its impact was considerable.

The issue raised such strong feelings that the first, tentative moves were made by some groups of Puritans towards setting up their own church for their own congregation. This Separatism would find no favour with either the Queen or her bishops. It effectively broke the usual channels of control. It also smacked of Anabaptism: the term used to describe a radical Protestant movement whose members rejected infant baptism in favour of the baptism of adults. Anabaptism was generally seen by secular governments as destructive of all government and all personal property. This was because Anabaptists took Separatism to its logical conclusion in denying that the State had any right to wield authority over the elect (those chosen by God for salvation). By refusing to pay tithes, take oaths of loyalty or perform military service, continental Anabaptists had provoked much persecution. So, when Bishop Grindal and other members of the High Commission found themselves facing a group of London Separatists in 1567, the spectre of Anabaptism was present in their minds. The following extracts are taken from the examination of members of this Plumber's Hall congregation:

1 *Grindal*: But have you not the gospel truly preached, and the sacraments ministered accordingly, and good order kept, although we differ from other churches in ceremonies, and in indifferent things, which lie in the prince's power to command for order's sake?
5 *Smith*: Indeed, as you said even now, for preaching and ministering the sacraments, so long as we might have the word freely preached, and the sacraments administered without the preferring of idolatrous gear above it, we never assembled together in houses ...
  Grindal: You see me wear a cope or a surplice in Paul's. I had rather min-
10 ister without these things, but for order's sake and obedience to the prince.
  Nixon: Your garments are accursed as they are used.
  Grindal: Where do you find them forbidden in the scriptures?
  Nixon: Where is the mass forbidden in the scriptures?
15 *Grindal*: All the learned are against you, will you be tried by them?
  White: We will be tried by the word of God ...

Archbishop Parker urged the Queen to endorse the *Advertisements* officially, but she refused. It is tempting to argue that this shows the Queen's culpable lack of interest in the Church, together with an almost malicious desire to force her bishops into confrontations and then refuse to back them up. However, we should remember that Parker was not following precisely the details on clerical dress as laid down in the Injunctions. It could be argued that the Queen was not prepared to support the bishops in imposing what she regarded as a breach of a settlement which she desired to be permanent.

There is little doubt that the Vestiarian Controversy provoked intense debate about the validity of episcopacy as an institution. Calvin had been quite prepared to recognise the English bishops as part of a reformed Church, but his successor in Geneva, Beza, disputed their necessity. It is no coincidence that, early in 1570, the Puritan minister and academic Thomas Cartwright should use his position at Cambridge University to launch an attack on the system of episcopacy, which he condemned as unscriptural. Cartwright also suggested an alternative form of church government, which will be discussed in detail in Chapter 3.

7 Elizabeth as Supreme Governor of the Church of England

> **KEY ISSUE** How far did Elizabeth act as a 'nursing mother' of the Church of England?

So far, it has been suggested that the Queen viewed the religious settlement with her own political needs at the forefront of her mind. What is lacking is an assessment of the way in which she used her role as Supreme Governor. How, in short, did she treat her Church?

To answer this question, we should start by examining the theory of Supreme Governorship, and then look at how Elizabeth interpreted her governorship in practice. In 1562, Jewel wrote his *An Apology or Answer in defence of the Church of England.* This piece of propaganda was written in response to Catholic taunts that the Church of England was nothing more than a mere parliamentary religion, whose lay head – the Queen – was, quite wrongly, able to decide on spiritual matters. Jewel's defence was twofold. Firstly, he cited Old Testament examples of monarchs who served God by watching over and protecting the faith, rebuking religious leaders where necessary and pointing out to them the errors of their ways. Secondly, he used passages from the book of Isaiah which referred to queens being the 'nursing mothers' of the faithful. Jewel also assumed that the Queen's title did not permit her to interfere in purely doctrinal matters, which were the responsibility of the clergy.

We can take the various elements of Jewel's concept of the godly ruler, and see how far they apply to Elizabeth. It is certainly open to doubt whether or not the Queen effectively protected the church. We have already noted her use of the Act of Exchange for financial gain. The historian Felicity Heal[5] has revealed how Elizabeth expected her bishops to provide church lands whenever she needed to reward courtiers and lacked the desire or resources to do so herself. With the exception of Cox and Sandys, few bishops stood up to her demands. The generation of bishops following the demise of the exiles seldom murmured at her financial exactions, which increased in the 1570s under the double stimulus of inflation and threat of foreign invasion. Nor would Elizabeth protect the Church against the similar demands of influential nobles. As we have seen, the second part of the Act of Exchange proved useful to the nobles, as the Queen pressured the bishops into granting them long and profitable leases on church land. In an era where land gave power and social status, her failure to defend the estates of her bishops did not assist their prestige. There is plenty of other evidence to suggest that the Queen was only too ready to place her own financial interests before the justified needs of her bishops for security and lay respect. Her officials were rigorous in their taxation demands, and, with the bishops forced to take responsibility for the tax returns to the exchequer for their dioceses, many ended up in debt to the Crown. This had not been an uncommon occurrence in the reigns of Edward VI and Mary. The difference is that, whereas her predecessors had been relatively sympathetic to the bishops, Elizabeth was not. The case of Bishop Parkhurst is a good example of the Queen's ruthlessness. Through no fault of his own, his diocese accumulated vast debts, which Elizabeth insisted on recovering. The result was that he had to leave his episcopal palace and live in retirement: not the best situation, one might think, from which to discharge his pastoral responsibility.

It is hard to avoid the conclusion that the Queen seldom acted as the 'nursing mother of the Church'. At best, she was a very selfish parent, concerned with her own needs and authority and rarely responding to the needs of her offspring. In Chapter 3 there is a discussion of one instance that reveals all too clearly Elizabeth's priorities. She suspended from the exercise of his pastoral office none other than her Archbishop of Canterbury – Parker's successor, Edmund Grindal. Significantly, the issue was preaching and mass meetings. Grindal had refused to implement her instruction to suppress 'prophesyings', which were large-scale gatherings of clergy and laity aimed at promoting a better-educated and more effective preaching ministry. Elizabeth, of course, saw them as potentially subversive. Jewel's image of the godly ruler rebuking the priesthood when it failed the people is here somewhat distorted. The Queen certainly did not hesitate to rebuke the priesthood – when it failed her.

Did the Queen interfere in doctrinal matters? The answer must be yes, but her involvement was generally of a negative type. Constantly at the back of her mind was the potential danger of allowing clerics to define doctrine in a rigid manner. What she could not afford politically was for numbers of people to be effectively excluded from the Church by a particularly narrow set of articles of belief. We remember her influence over the wording on the Eucharist in the 1559 Book of Common Prayer which allowed for a number of possible interpretations. In 1563, Archbishop Parker, working through Convocation (the clerical parliament), produced the Thirty-nine Articles: a definitive statement of church doctrine. Some – but by no means all – articles reflected standard Calvinist ideas. Article 17, for example, spoke of the sweet comfort offered to the soul by the concept of predestination, where salvation was predetermined rather than attained through one's godly behaviour. Elizabeth had no role in the writing of the Thirty-nine Articles, but, significantly, refused to allow them to be confirmed by Act of Parliament. This was not necessarily because she disapproved of most of the theology, but rather because the

Articles included strongly-worded condemnations of Catholic practices. She clearly felt that such attacks were likely to cause resentment
among her Catholic subjects. However, once the Pope had excommunicated Elizabeth and sought her deposition in 1570, she allowed
Parliament to confirm the Articles. Catholics were being identified as
potential traitors and therefore did not need to be appeased.

8 The Elizabethan Religious Settlement: Some Conclusions

This chapter has sought to explain the nature of the Elizabethan religious settlement. This has involved examining, not only what the settlement actually was in terms of the doctrine and organisation of the
Church of England, but also whose views and needs were reflected in
it. We have also been interested in finding out the extent to which the
settlement remained consistent throughout the reign.

It is clear that the most important single factor in explaining the
settlement is the Queen herself. That it was a Protestant settlement
rather than a Catholic one reflected her religious views as well as
those of her most loyal supporters. That the Church of England
employed a Catholic-style hierarchy, retained certain practices reminiscent of Catholicism and was administered by a clergy whose
appearance was also largely traditional, reflected Elizabeth's percep-
tion of her political needs. As we shall see in Chapter 4, Elizabeth
intended to let Catholicism in England die out slowly in preference to
stamping it out, which would have created discord and disunity.

It might be argued that the Elizabethan settlement of religion was
largely Erastian. This means that it was intended primarily to serve the
needs of the State, and to subordinate the clergy to secular authority.
This is a useful argument up to a point. After all, the evidence in
Chapter 2 certainly tends to support the view that Elizabeth consist-
ently used the Church with political concerns uppermost in her mind.
However, it would be a mistake to see this as simply Erastian, because
what Elizabeth had in mind was less the needs of an abstraction like
the State than the needs of Elizabeth I, Queen of England. Her own
authority was to be jealously guarded through and against her
bishops. Her financial needs were to be met by exploiting episcopal
lands. And her fear of uncontrolled gatherings was to predominate
over the needs of her Church. Small wonder that she defended her
settlement against change or development, since it was so much a part
of herself.

References
1   R. Ashton, *Reformation and Revolution 1558–1660* (London, 1985), p. 75
2   N. Jones in C. Haigh (ed.), *The Reign of Elizabeth I* (London, 1984)

3 J.E. Neale, *Queen Elizabeth I* (Harmondsworth, 1960)
4 P. Collinson, *The Elizabethan Puritan Movement* (Oxford, 1967)
5 F. Heal in F. Heal and R.O'Day (eds.), *Church and Society in England: Henry VIII to James I* (London, 1977)

Summary Diagram
The Elizabethan Religious Settlement

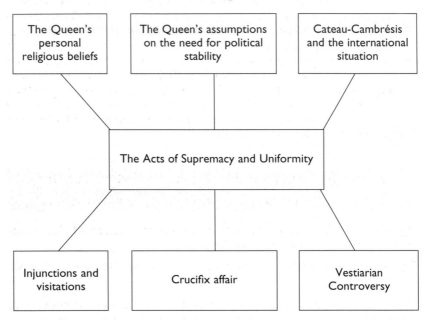

Working on Chapter 2

When you are making detailed notes on this chapter, avoid simple lists of 'what happened'. As always in history, information has little value on its own: it should be used to serve an argument. So, make sure you write with the following questions in mind: (i) What factors shaped the settlement? (ii) How did the terms of the settlement reflect those factors? (iii) How and why did the Queen defend the settlement? The Key Issues will feed into these questions. In general, diagrammatic notes have much to commend them. Spider diagrams in particular allow you to explore the links between themes and force you to come up with headings which by their very nature demonstrate an understanding of the topic. It would be a good idea to produce such diagrams for this chapter. You could then do one (admittedly large!) diagram to cover questions (i) and (ii), which would allow you to explore the vital links between them.

Answering structured and essay questions on the Elizabethan religious settlement

Questions will, in all probability, focus on the nature of the settlement. You might, for example, be asked:

a) How far did political considerations shape the Elizabethan religious settlement?

This question can come in various guises. You could, of course, be asked how far religious ideals shaped the settlement – or how far it was shaped by the personal needs of Elizabeth herself. In each case, you need to bear the following in mind.

It is always a good idea to define key terms in an introduction to an essay. It would certainly be advisable to define 'Elizabethan religious settlement' (see the introduction to this chapter). Elizabeth's personal needs would also need definition. They would encompass both her own personal religious beliefs and her political needs. It is, incidentally, as well to learn the word 'erastian', which means 'to serve the needs of the state'. It is arguably unfair for an examiner to use the word in a question, but by no means unreasonable to expect good candidates to exploit it.

Good essays are the product of good plans. A good plan allows the student to unpack the question, identify the appropriate information and to decide which factors are the most significant in an explanation/argument (usually known as the 'hierarchy of factors'). I strongly recommend that you attempt a plan for essays a), b) and c).

b) How far do you agree with the view that the Elizabethan religious settlement owed little to Elizabeth herself?
c) How far did religious considerations shape the Elizabethan religious settlement?

3 Elizabeth and the Puritans

POINTS TO CONSIDER

One of the most important issues is that of definition. The advice in the *Answering structured and essay questions* section of the previous chapter suggested that it was vital to define key terms. It is particularly important in this chapter to make use of the threefold definition of the word 'puritan'. In general, examiners are keen to ask you to consider how far Puritans posed a threat to the Elizabethan religious settlement. This can only be answered effectively if you distinguish between the different types of Puritan.

KEY DATES

1571 Cartwright's pro-Presbyterian Lectures.
'Alphabet' bills.
1572 John Field's *Admonitions to Parliament*.
Massacre of St Bartholomew's Day.
1575 Edmund Grindal made Archbishop of Canterbury.
1576 Grindal refused the Queen's instruction to suppress prophesyings.
1577 Grindal suspended.
1582 Robert Browne published the Separatist *Treatise of Reformation without tarrying for any*.
1583 Death of Grindal.
John Whitgift appointed Archbishop of Canterbury.
Three Articles.
1584 Turner's pro-Presbyterian bill.
1587 Cope's pro-Presbyterian bill.
1588 *Martin Marprelate* tracts.
1593 Richard Hooker's *Of the Laws of Ecclesiastical Polity*.
1595 Lambeth Articles.

1 Introduction

KEY ISSUE In what ways were the three types of Puritan a) similar and b) dissimilar?

In Shakespeare's play *Twelfth Night*, the upper-class louts Sir Toby Belch and Sir Andrew Aguecheek have a discussion about a man by the name of Malvolio. On hearing that Malvolio is 'sometimes a kind of Puritan', Sir Andrew comments: 'O! If I thought that, I'd beat him like a dog.' The same character remarks to Malvolio himself: 'Dost thou think, because thou art virtuous, there shall be no cakes and ale?' Aguecheek's attitude gives an insight into one meaning of the word 'Puritan', a nickname which became current from the 1560s. Shakespeare is not alone among playwrights in presenting Puritans as kill-joys: they also appear in plays by other writers as hypocrites with a strong line in sexual repression. This kind of abuse is not restricted to writers who might have felt their livelihoods threatened. It also appears in a learned controversy in the 1570s between the future Archbishop of Canterbury, John Whitgift, and his Puritan opponent, Thomas Cartwright. For good measure, Whitgift also accused Puritans of being heretical in their obsession with 'purity' in their personal conduct, and divisive in their alleged refusal to associate with those who disagreed with them. Puritans, by this token, were dangerous opponents of all lawful authority.

'Puritanism', then, is a term that historians must use with considerable care. Any word originating in abuse is as likely to tell you as much – or as little – about the abuser as it does about the abused. Moreover, since the term was applied so widely and incautiously in the sixteenth century, the historian must take particular care both to define Puritanism and then to outline crucial differences of viewpoint among those who would, however reluctantly, accept that the name 'Puritan' applied to them. To assume that all Puritans had identical attitudes is about as sensible as assuming that all teenagers think and behave in the same way. Obviously, Puritans had certain shared values and ideas, but this does not necessarily mean that Puritanism was a unified movement. Elizabethan Puritanism cannot be handled in a meaningful way unless a preliminary attempt is made to work out what Puritans had in common and what divided them. Only then can we deal with the questions that have been of particular interest to historians: namely, 'How strong was Puritanism?', 'How greatly did it influence the Elizabethan Church of England?' and 'How much of a challenge did it represent to the Elizabethan religious settlement?'

Our first task, then, is to establish what Puritans had in common. In this book, the term 'Puritanism' was introduced on page 23 in the course of a discussion of Sir John Neale's supposed 'Puritan Choir'. In this context, it meant Protestants who were influenced by the 'godly society' of Calvin's Geneva and who wished to push the Elizabethan religious settlement as far as possible in that direction. This is a useful starting point. In theology, a Puritan would certainly be Calvinist. He would also be strongly anti-Catholic, and so would wish to remove everything from the Church which was reminiscent of Catholicism. For the greater glory of God, he would wish to control social behaviour. This discipline was necessary because Puritans viewed mankind as being sinful and weak. Life on earth was not for frivolity, for enjoyment or for the display of wealth, but was for the fulfilment of God's commands. Finally, a Puritan would place great emphasis on the preaching of God's Word. In this most vital of tasks, ministers (Puritans did not use the word 'priest') were expected to explain to their congregations what God demanded of His people.

However, it should be remembered that the danger with convenient generalisations is that they often hide profound differences. Such an all-embracing definition of a Puritan is a case in point. There were, as we shall see, many who can and should be labelled 'Puritan' and yet who were divided so fundamentally on some issues that they regarded each other with fear and hatred.

One of the historian's most important tasks is to impose order on the manifold confusions of the past. In this context, it is helpful (although it was not done by contemporaries) to identify three different types of Puritan who accepted the central assumptions of Puritanism but whose differences were no less real: the 'Conformist', the 'Presbyterian' and the 'Separatist'. This categorisation will be used throughout this chapter. But remember that it is a modern system of labelling: many Elizabethans would certainly have recognised the terms 'Presbyterian' and 'Separatist', although they may not have had very precise meanings for them. 'Conformist' was likely to have had a significantly different meaning.

For our purposes, we should identify the 'Conformist' as a Puritan who certainly accepted the major aspects of the wider Puritan position, but who was prepared to compromise on what he saw as less essential elements. Calvinist theology, the centrality of preaching and the importance of 'discipline' were at the heart of the Conformist's Protestantism. However, he was also prepared to give due weight to other factors. He recognised that there were aspects of the Elizabethan religious settlement that were distasteful to his conscience, yet he was prepared to bite on the bullet in the interests of the national Church, of uniformity and of loyalty to the Queen. The Catholic-style hierarchy and clerical dress of the Church of England might be offensive, but they were bearable.

It is essential to recognise that Puritanism and the Elizabethan Church of England were not necessarily mutually exclusive. It was possible to be a Puritan and to work within the Church. It was also possible to rise to the very top of the hierarchy, and yet retain those central assumptions of Puritanism. But what was possible was not always easy. This will become all too clear when we examine the career of Edmund Grindal as Archbishop of Canterbury in section 3. Conformists frequently found the compromises hard to swallow, especially when they discovered that Elizabeth had no intention of moving beyond the letter of the Acts of Uniformity and Supremacy. But to argue that all Puritans were out to subvert or destroy Elizabeth's Church of England would be a travesty. We cannot count the number of Conformist Puritans, but we know they were there. This chapter will discuss a number of incidents which amounted to confrontation between Puritans and the bishops when the latter chose or were forced to insist on the full observation of the settlement. What is significant is the readiness of many Puritan clergy to accept compromises when offered, rather than to follow some of their fellows into opposition to the Elizabethan Church of England.

To the Puritans known as Presbyterians, such compromise was unacceptable. The Church was, in their eyes, fatally flawed because it employed a Catholic-style hierarchy of archbishops and bishops. Where in the Bible, they asked, were these titles and offices to be found? No answer was expected, of course: there are no explicit references to archbishops and bishops in Scripture. Opponents might argue that the Bible gave no clear indication of the structure of the Church anyway. But the Presbyterians denied this. They felt that the system used by the Apostles *could* be identified from the New Testament. To fail to use it was nothing less than a rejection of the authority of Scripture. Presbyterians argued that God required a church organisation based on the government of each congregation by ministers and lay elders. Indeed, the term 'Presbyterianism' is derived from the word meaning 'elder'. It was claimed that this system was particularly effective in imposing the discipline which was central to Puritanism. Ministers and elders could lead the congregation into a godly way of life through example, through counselling, through criticism – both mutual and personal – and through spiritual punishments like excommunication. Presbyterians could point to Geneva and say that this system worked. Where else in the world did such courtesy, such good order and such godliness prevail?

All this does not mean that congregations were to be independent of each other. To the Presbyterian, such independence would lead to chaos. Instead, he demanded a national system whereby individual congregations sent representatives to regional and national meetings (or 'synods'). The uniform doctrine and discipline decided there would then be taken back to, and imposed on, the local churches. What need, therefore, for bishops and archbishops? They stemmed from man, and man was corrupt. But presbyters, it was claimed, derived from God. Who would argue for the corruptness of God?

If Presbyterianism sought to discard the authority of bishops and archbishops over the Church, where did it leave the authority of the monarch? The short answer is, somewhat uncertain and exposed. It is difficult to see how the Queen, for example, could effectively control a Church organised in this manner. In fact, such a system separated the Church from secular authority in a radical way. Major landowners – especially since the Henrician Reformation – had become used to exercising a right to appoint clergymen of their choosing to churches on their own lands. This right had been inherited along with land bought at the time of the dissolution of the monasteries. But the Presbyterian system gave the right of appointment to the elders, with or without advice from the synods.

Presbyterianism, then, was uncompromisingly a national system. But some Puritans refused to accept any form of ecclesiastical authority which failed to coincide with their *individual* understanding of Scripture. This led logically to the independent congregation of the Separatists, where a group formed its own Church, not on the basis of the need for national or even regional unity, but on the basis of a doctrine agreed by the members of a single congregation. Discipline could still be imposed, because members marked their agreement by entering into a contract – a covenant – which bound them to that shared interpretation. This kind of Church frequently looked for a role model to the persecutions of early Christians at the time when true believers were in a minority. There were also plenty of biblical passages to show that believers should expect such persecution. This was probably just as well, because Separatists were bound to be persecuted. Those in authority assumed that Separatism was the first step towards the overthrow of all established order. It seemed to break down traditional loyalties to social as well as to religious superiors.

Three major types of Puritan within the England of Elizabeth have been identified: the 'Conformist', the 'Presbyterian' and the 'Separatist'. However, one must not assume that these three types are rigid in the sense that Puritans were unable to move between or in and out of these varying attitudes towards the Church. Nor would the Protestant who found the Elizabethan religious settlement very much to his taste necessarily be antagonistic to all manifestations of Puritanism.

This discussion of the different types of Puritan has so far lacked one essential element: how did Puritanism develop? The 'Conformist', 'Presbyterian' and 'Separatist' were unlikely to spring to life, fully-fledged, in instantaneous response to the Acts of Uniformity and Supremacy. It therefore makes sense to examine the development of Puritanism in a basically chronological manner.

2 Puritanism and Presbyterianism in the 1570s

> **KEY ISSUES** The ideas of Cartwright: why was he dismissed from Cambridge University? What led to the imprisonment of John Field? Why was the impact of Presbyterian ideas so limited at this time?

In dealing with the growth of early Presbyterianism, it is important to recognise that the development of the movement cannot be traced just to one individual or just to one incident. This is not to deny the importance of a theorist such as Thomas Cartwright, whose lectures at Cambridge University represented the first influential public demand for a Presbyterian system. But it is also vital to understand that Presbyterian ideas became attractive to some Puritans when they felt themselves to be the victims of persecution at the hands of bishops.

In Cartwright's spring lectures of 1570, he contrasted the hierarchy and discipline of the Church of England with that of the Apostolic Church. Needless to say, the former was found wanting. In particular, Cartwright called for the abolition of the titles and offices of archbishops, bishops, deans and archdeacons. He also argued that the minister should be elected by his congregation. In effect, Cartwright was suggesting a full-scale Presbyterian system, including district assemblies known as *classes* (pronounced 'class-eeze') as well as provincial and national synods. These were to be responsible for both doctrine and discipline. A system of this type left little or no place for the Supreme Governorship. No doubt this is why Cartwright's lectures skirted the issue of the Queen's authority over the Church. They did, however, cost Cartwright his professorial chair. He left for Geneva where he could see a system in operation which bore a distinct resemblance to his vision of the Apostolic Church.

There is, however, no evidence that a Presbyterian movement developed as a result of Cartwright's lectures. Indeed, it is clear that other centres of radical Puritanism were inclined to accept – albeit reluctantly – the authority of the traditional hierarchy. But this conformism was not the result of carefully considered compromise. Instead, it depended on the local bishop not asking awkward questions about how far Puritan ministers were conforming to the Act of Uniformity. However, the activities of some Puritans did suggest to the bishops the need to conduct such checks. In particular, there was considerable episcopal resentment when Puritan tactics in Parliament led – unintentionally – to the loss of important reforming legislation. In the session of 1571, the bishops had hoped to see certain bills (known as the 'Alphabet Bills') pass through Parliament to curb the evils of ministers holding more than one parish living, or failing to reside in their own parish (abuses known as 'pluralism' and 'absenteeism'). But the Puritan MP William Strickland had tried to yoke that legislation to a Prayer Book Bill of his own devising. This bill attempted to do away with certain practices reminiscent of Catholicism, such as the use of the surplice and kneeling at Communion. All it achieved, however, was the Queen's indignation. In her view, Parliament had no right to tamper with the religious settlement. She simply vetoed most of the Alphabet Bills. The bishops, not unnaturally, were inclined to blame Puritans for the loss of useful reforms. Their response was to increase pressure on Puritans to conform. To do this, use was made of Convocation's right to grant or renew the licences without which no clergyman could preach. Licences were not to be renewed unless the minister gave full and unconditional subscription to the Thirty-nine Articles. On top of this, certain influential Puritan ministers were summoned before the Ecclesiastical Commissioners and told they must subscribe, not only to the Articles, but also to the Book of Common Prayer and to the surplice.

Among those summoned was the young clergyman John Field, a man who was to play a central role in the attempt to organise a Presbyterian church system for England. It is significant that Field did his best to respond with some form of compromise: a sign that he was not, at this stage, out to reject the authority or role of the episcopate. He offered a qualified subscription to the Articles and Prayer Book and, although he could not bring himself to wear the surplice, he promised not to condemn those who did. But his offer was rejected. Early in 1572, he was forbidden to preach.

Field's response to this ban reflects his bitterness. In 1572 he co-wrote and published manifestos which were nothing less than a public attack on the institution of episcopacy. The first of the two *Admonitions to Parliament* accused the bishops of being enemies of true Christianity. Presbyterianism was advanced as the only form of church government and discipline to be supported by Scripture. Below is an extract:

1 May it therefore please your wisdoms to understand, we in England are so far off from having a Church rightly reformed, according to the prescript of God's word that as yet we are not come to the outward face of the same ... Let us now come to the .. part, which concerneth eccle-

5 siastical discipline. The officers that have to deal in this charge are chiefly three: ministers ... elders; and deacons. Concerning elders, not only their office but their name is out of this English Church utterly removed. Instead ... the pope has brought in, and we yet maintain, the lordship of one man over many churches ... The final end of this disci-

10 pline is the reforming of the disordered and to bring them to repentance and to bridle such as would offend. The chiefest part and last punishment of this discipline is excommunication, by the consent of the Church determined ... In the primitive Church it was in many men's hands; now alone one excommunicateth ... now it is pronounced for

15 every light trifle. Then excommunication was greatly regarded and feared; now, because it is a money matter, no whit at all esteemed.

Attached to this Admonition was Field's *A View of Popish Abuses yet remaining in the English Church*. Field clearly intended to pull no punches. This work listed the articles to which the author and others had been instructed to subscribe. The first was that the Book of Common Prayer contained nothing 'repugnant to' the Word of God. Field commented:

1 We must needs say as followeth, that this book is an unperfect book, culled and picked out of that popish dunghill, the Mass book full of all abominations ... By the word of God, it [the minister's office] is an office of preaching, they make it an office of reading: Christ said go

5 preach, they in mockery give them the Bible, and authority to preach, and yet suffer them not, except that they have new licences ... In this

book we are enjoined to receive the Communion kneeling, which ...
has in it a show of popish idolatry ... The public baptism, that also is
full of childish and superstitious toys ... they do superstitiously and
10 wickedly institute a new sacrament, which is proper to Christ only,
marking the child in the forehead with a cross ...

Field spent a year in prison as a result of his literary efforts, but it is
unlikely that he was thought of as a martyr. The vehemence of his
opinions and the savagery of his attack on the bishops appalled many
Puritans, including the older generation represented by the Marian
exiles. The impact on Parliament was slight. The House of
Commons, rather than follow the lead of the Admonition, preferred
to adopt a deferential approach. The Commons tended to present
petitions to the Queen rather than introduce bills which would
simply be vetoed. Archbishop Parker took the opportunity to use the
subscription weapon against as many Puritans as he saw fit, but there
were a number of reasons why the hierarchy of the Church and the
Puritans were by no means irreconcilable enemies. Firstly, all
Protestants were united in horror at the St Bartholomew's Day massacre of Huguenots (French Protestants) in Paris in 1572. Secondly,
the Puritans were not without friends in very high places. Robert
Dudley, Earl of Leicester – the Queen's favourite – and his brother,
the Earl of Warwick, were well known as patrons to many a godly
preacher. Thirdly, the translation of Edmund Grindal from the
Archbishopric of York to that of Canterbury in 1575 meant that a
known and respected reformer was at the helm. Could episcopalian
government forge an alliance with Puritans and deflect attention
away from Presbyterianism?

3 The Tragedy of Grindal

KEY ISSUES Why did Grindal oppose the Queen's instructions?
How far does his opposition suggest a threat to the Elizabethan
religious settlement on the part of the so-called 'conformist'
Puritans?

The word 'tragedy' should not be used lightly. Its use implies an emotional involvement in the fate of Grindal: the kind of involvement an
historian should generally avoid. And yet, it is hard not to feel sympathy for a decent man who was asked – or instructed – to make one
compromise too many.

Chapter 2 included a brief account of the sorry end of Grindal's
effective career as Archbishop, brought about when the Queen suspended him following his refusal to stop the so-called 'prophesyings'
(see page 34). This episode must be looked at in greater detail, since
it helps us to answer important questions. Was the Queen correct in

seeing these meetings as a threat to her authority? Why was the issue so important to Grindal that he was prepared to sacrifice his position? Seeking an answer to these questions provides insight, not only into the nature of Grindal's relationship with Puritanism, but also into the extent to which Puritanism was revolutionary.

There is evidence to suggest that, at the start of Grindal's episcopal career, he took on the role of bishop only after considerable heart-searching. Like many other Marian exiles, Grindal had kept up a correspondence with influential continental reformers. An exchange of letters with Peter Martyr in Zurich reveals that Grindal had accepted that his elevation as Bishop of London would involve him in some regrettable compromises. He argued, however, that compromise was permissible so long as it did not affect the salvation of those in the minister's care. Grindal, it should be recalled, did not care for the use of the surplice. But he was prepared to accept the right of the Queen to enforce it because it was no handicap to the teaching of true doctrine. The concept of *adiaphora*, or matters external to salvation, was therefore of great value to him as he strove to reconcile his role as bishop and archbishop in a national Church with his role as a guide for souls. His high office was important to him. After all, if he refused the office, might not other, less suitable, men take it on?

Grindal clearly expected his clergy to share his stance on matters external to salvation. As Bishop of London, he was initially reluctant to impose the surplice where it caused genuine distress among his clergy. However, when pressed to do so, he became impatient of ministers who tried both to keep their livings and to ignore the necessary demands of secular and spiritual authority.

Grindal's willingness to accept the right of the Queen to demand uniformity over minor matters should not, therefore, be seen as weakness or pliability. Instead, he represents the position of the 'Conformist' Puritans. But, as we shall see, this was not an easy position to maintain. When he saw his central principles threatened – the principles shared by all Puritans – Grindal stood fast. The 'prophesyings' storm should be put into the context of Grindal's undoubted interest in clerical education and his view of the vital importance of securing effective preachers. Grindal expended much time and effort both in inquiring into the learning of candidates for the ministry and also in conducting visitations (inspections) of the clergy within his archdiocese. The problem for him was that he saw the Queen's demand that he crush prophesyings as an attack on a vital tool in improving the effectiveness of the very preaching ministry on which the evangelising of England depended. It has already been noted that this commitment to preaching was a characteristic of Puritanism.

How far were prophesyings a threat to the 1559 settlement? The term itself seems to imply the wild and unbridled enthusiasm of would-be visionaries and prophets. In fact, these meetings were gatherings of clergy where preachers could practise their skills and obtain an assessment of their performance and orthodoxy from their colleagues. The 'exercise' was performed under the supervision of a moderator, who was usually a respected practitioner in the art of preaching. Its value to the inexperienced or ill-educated clergyman was enormous. As Professor Collinson has pointed out,[1] prophesyings were seen as the 'universities of the poor ministers'. After all, did not the Royal Injunctions of 1559 require non-graduate ministers to study the Scriptures and other works? The 'exercise' generally started with two or three sermons on the same text preached in front of a mixed clerical and lay audience. After the sermons came a conference from which laymen were excluded. Preachers were here given the opinion of the moderator and others on their sermons. The effect of such regular fortnightly or monthly exercises was bound to improve the morale of the clergy as well as their professional expertise. This is why many prophesyings had taken place with the full support of the bishops, who had appointed moderators, instructed them to enforce attendance and published orders of the proceedings. This also serves as a reminder that, while prophesyings would indeed appeal to Puritans of all types, non-Puritans were not unaware of their value. Prophesyings were certainly not a uniquely Presbyterian weapon, whatever vague similarity the meeting might have to a synod. Very possibly the Queen thought otherwise. Local meetings lacking in the firm and consistent direction provided by bishops may have implied, in her mind, lack of uniformity, and lack of uniformity was a threat both to the Supreme Governorship and to the stability of the realm. As Chapter 2 revealed, the Queen was generally hostile to evangelism which would, in the short term, provoke resentment from those who were more conservative in religious matters. And resentment was a potent disturber of the peace.

It would seem, perhaps, that the Queen had little real cause to fear prophesyings as a factor stimulating disunity. On the other hand, it is true that some prophesyings did appear to reflect Separatist tendencies. Goings-on of this sort at Southam in Warwickshire came to the ear of the Queen, and Leicester, along with Burghley and Walsingham, attempted to defuse the situation. They warned Grindal of the need to make sure that the local bishop was fully aware of what was taking place. Bishop Bentham, it seems, had known little or nothing about the Southam exercise. However, it is clear that Grindal, for one, felt that the value of prophesyings considerably outweighed their potential dangers. When, in 1576, the Queen demanded that Grindal suppress all prophesyings and restrict the number of preachers to three or four per shire, his response was to canvass the opinion of his fellow bishops on the value of godly exercises. Out of 15 bishops, 10 approved with various degrees of qualification. Only one saw them as a threat to the episcopate. This bishop, Scory of Hereford, argued that they were the first step towards Presbyterianism. But Scory's diocese was notoriously conservative, and his knowledge of Puritanism in any form was correspondingly limited. Grindal's resulting letter to the Queen defended prophesy-ings, discussed ways of making sure they were rigorously controlled and, in the end, implied that Elizabeth must be aware of the need to please God rather than herself. Below is an extract from Grindal's letter:

1 The speeches which it hath pleased you to deliver unto me, when I last attended on your highness, concerning abridging the number of preachers, and the utter suppression of all learned exercises and con-ferences among the ministers of the Church ... have exceedingly dis-
5 mayed and discomforted me ... Howsoever report hath been made to your Majesty concerning these exercises, yet I and others of your bishops ... having found by experience that these profits and com-modities following hath ensued of them:
I. The ministers of the Church are more skilful and ready in the scrip-
10 tures, and apter to teach their flocks.
... III. Some afore suspected in doctrine are brought hereby to open confession of the truth.
IV. Ignorant ministers are driven to study, if not for conscience yet for shame and fear of discipline.
15 V. The opinion of laymen touching the idleness of the clergy is hereby removed.
Only backward men in religion ... do fret against it ... And although some few have abused this good and necessary exercise, there is no reason that the malice of a few should prejudice all ...
20 And now being sorry, that I have been so long and tedious to your majesty, I will draw to an end, most humbly praying the same well to consider these two short petitions following. The first is, that you would refer all these ecclesiastical matters ... unto the bishops and divines of your realm ... For indeed they are things to be judged, as an
25 ancient father writeth: 'In the church, or a synod, not in a palace.' ... Remember, madam, that you are a mortal creature. 'Look not only ... upon the purple and princely array ...' Is it not dust and ashes?

Flattery, it seems, was not a weapon in Grindal's armoury. Uncompromising, almost threatening, in the way it reminded Elizabeth of the accountability of her actions before God – this was not a letter seeking to advise, but one informing the Queen, not only of her duty, but also of the limits of her power. There were precedents in the history of the early Church for bishops lecturing their mon-archs, but Elizabeth was too angry to care to refresh her memory on ecclesiastical history. Grindal, it seems, would accept little help in the storm that followed. His friends in the Privy Council tried to find some sort of compromise between the Archbishop and the enraged Queen, but Grindal would not budge. The Queen gave instructions for ways to be found of depriving Grindal of his office, but there was, as Burghley remarked, no precedent for the removal of an archbishop in these circumstances. Grindal was under virtual house-arrest in his palace at Lambeth, and was suspended from his duties. There followed five years in which Grindal could do nothing for the Church on whose behalf he had made such a courageous – if ill-advised – stand. Only his death in 1583 brought the sorry tale to an end. As for the prophesyings, Elizabeth wrote directly to the bishops:

1   Right reverent father in God, we greet you well. We hear to our great grief that in sundry parts of our realm there are no small number of persons ... which, contrary to our laws established for the public divine service of Almighty God and the administration of His holy sacraments
5   within this Church of England, do daily devise, imagine, propound and put into execution sundry new rites and forms ... as well by procuring unlawful assemblies of a great number of our people out of their ordinary parishes ... which manner of invasions they in some places call prophesying and in some other places exercises ... we will and straitly
10 charge you that you ... charge the same forthwith to cease ... but if any shall attempt, or continue, or renew the same, we will you not only to commit them unto prison as maintainers of disorders, but also to advertise to us or our Council of the names and qualities of them and of their maintainers and abettors ... And in these things we charge you to he so
15 careful and vigilant, as by your negligence, if we shall hear of any person attempting to offend ... without your correction or information to us, we be not forced to make some example or reformation of you, according to your deserts.

The result of the Queen's action was indeed a clampdown on prophesyings, but there were ways and means of ministers getting together to hear and discuss sermons without calling them prophesyings. If, for example, there was one 'lecture' rather than a number of sermons, then this still left the clergy the opportunity to meet together to discuss it. Some larger towns appointed their own lecturer, or clergy found market days ideal for hearing the sermons of visiting rural ministers. Of course, this kind of meeting appealed to the converted, and therefore lacked the capacity of the prophesyings to improve clerical education in general.

Grindal's fate demonstrates the difficulties facing the 'Conformist' Puritan. The concept of *adiaphora* was sufficient to permit Conformists to accept with a reasonably good grace the rituals and ornaments of the Church of England. But when the Queen's actions threatened their most central assumptions, then they were in trouble. It was a matter for individual conscience how far each Conformist was prepared to compromise further. Grindal had clearly reached the sticking point. One problem was that both parties in a compromise are usually expected to give a little ground. However, the Queen had no intention of deviating from her stance in the interests of anything at all, let alone of compromising. It is hard to escape the conclusion that the Queen's rigidity created avoidable problems. Conformist

Puritans were, like prophesyings, no real threat to the Elizabethan religious settlement if sympathetically handled.

4 Whitgift and the Puritans

KEY ISSUES What was the nature of Archbishop Whitgift's attack on Puritans? What effects did that attack have?

Following Grindal's death in 1583, the Queen appointed John Whitgift as his successor. He was a man with little or no sympathy for Puritanism in any form. It was convenient for the Queen that Whitgift also had a particularly well-developed sense of the importance of authority and uniformity. In his first major sermon as Archbishop, he called upon all parties who were discontented with the Elizabethan settlement – Catholics and Puritans alike – to obey their superiors. By superiors, he meant the bishops and the Queen. In examining Whitgift's career as Archbishop, it is important to consider two questions. Firstly, what was the effect of Whitgift's attack on Puritanism? Secondly, what conclusions can be reached on the strength of Puritanism in this latter part of the Queen's reign?

Whitgift's harsh and uncompromising approach is revealed in his attempt to impose his Three Articles of 1583 on all ministers. The first article required the minister to accept the Royal Supremacy. The second required him to agree that the Book of Common Prayer and the Ordinal contained nothing contrary to the Word of God. The Ordinal dealt with the ordination of bishops as well as ministers. Anyone accepting it would therefore also be accepting episcopacy as the right and proper system of church government. Thirdly, the subscriber had to acknowledge that the Thirty Nine Articles were similarly agreeable to the Word of God. Whitgift would accept nothing but complete and unreserved subscription. There were to be no deals, no turning of blind eyes to Puritans of uneasy conscience. The Archbishop's severity is also revealed in his instructions on how the Articles were to be administered. Clergy under suspicion were forced to take an oath that they would answer all questions truthfully. But they were not told beforehand what the questions would be. This was known as an *ex officio* oath, and was borrowed from civil law: its use in Church courts was without precedent. A minister might therefore be faced with a question such as 'Do you use the Book of Common Prayer without alteration?' and be forced to reply yea or nay. Small wonder that such inflexibility and aggression caused uproar. Within the dioceses covered by the province of Canterbury, at least 300 ministers were suspended for refusing to subscribe. The Privy Council, bombarded with protests from sympathetic gentry, advised Whitgift to accept a modified subscription. Whitgift followed this advice, and most of the recalcitrant ministers duly subscribed.

What was the effect of Whitgift's aggressive pressure for uniformity? On the face of it, it seems reasonable to argue that he unwittingly gave stimulus to the case for Presbyterianism. After all, being persecuted by an archbishop was hardly likely to arouse enthusiasm for episcopacy among Puritan ministers. There is, however, some difficulty in finding evidence to support this argument. One would need to establish the relative strengths of Presbyterianism before and after the arrival of Whitgift as Archbishop. But how? Convenient statistics are not to be had. Finding some other way to assess the strength of Presbyterianism before Whitgift is fraught with difficulties. By the time of Whitgift's translation to Canterbury, meetings of clergy which ignored diocesan boundaries were certainly taking place. Historians refer to these meetings as the Classical movement. The name derives from the term *classis* (plural, *classes*), meaning a regional meeting to which the local congregation sent its representatives for discussion of such issues as discipline. But danger lies in assuming that these *classes* were Cartwright-style Presbyterian synods. Firstly, there was no meaningful national framework of *classes*, whatever John Field and other Presbyterians would have wished. Secondly, not all those who took part in *classes* were committed Presbyterians. Often, these meetings were informal arenas for study and prayer, rather than synods in embryo. Thirdly, Presbyterianism demands a major role for lay elders, yet these meetings were usually attended only by the clergy. No doubt John Field hoped that the *classes* would respond to the resentment caused by Whitgift by stimulating the growth and expansion of Presbyterianism. But noisy propaganda from the likes of Field does not prove that Whitgift's Articles caused an influx of recruits to the Presbyterian position. Field – not for the last time – underestimated the desire of ministers to avoid radical positions and unseemly conflict. His message was simple: clergy should not offer any form of subscription to the Articles, conditional or otherwise. But what alternative did the ministers have if they wished to maintain their profession and to have influence over their parishioners? If Whitgift had really pushed clergy into opposition and Presbyterianism, why then did so few refuse to subscribe to the modified Articles? 'Conformist' Puritans, in the main, continued to conform.

Field did seek to exploit wider resentment at Whitgift's behaviour. He launched a nationwide survey to establish grievances against the bishops, in the hope that forthcoming parliaments could be influenced thereby to pass pro-Presbyterian legislation. However, despite the best efforts of Field and his sympathisers, the 1584 election was by no means a Puritan triumph. As the historian MacCulloch has pointed out,[2] even the supposed heartlands of Puritan influence like Essex failed to return the hoped-for godly MPs. Nevertheless, the Presbyterians did their best to sway Parliament. Secret presses issued manifestos, and a bill was introduced by Dr Peter Turner in 1584 which would have set up a national Presbyterian system. But the Queen could and did come up with her standard veto, using the powerful oratory of Sir Christopher Hatton to forbid the House to discuss religious matters.

In the Parliament of 1586–7, the Presbyterians tried again. Excitement over Leicester's Netherlands expedition (see page 105) and the Babington Plot (see page 141), together with the publication of the results of some of Field's surveys, may have contributed to the return of a larger number of MPs sympathetic to Puritanism in general (although not necessarily to Presbyterianism). Perhaps we are at last getting close to Professor Neale's elusive 'Puritan Choir' (see page 22). One of their number, Anthony Cope, offered for discussion 'a bill and a book' in February 1587. The bill proposed doing away with the Book of Common Prayer and replacing it with a version of the Genevan Prayer Book which incorporated a fully Presbyterian system of church government. Cope and some supporters were despatched to the Tower on Elizabeth's instructions, and government spokesmen brought their guns to bear on a bill and book which, in any case, had little or no chance of passing through Parliament with or without government intervention. As Christopher Hatton pointed out, a system of church organisation like that envisaged by Cope would threaten the influence of landowners over church livings. Even Sir Walter Mildmay, the founder of Emmanuel College, Cambridge – an institution dedicated to the training of Puritan ministers – had nothing good to say about this proposal. The fact that the House of Commons had given leave for Cope's bill to be read proves merely that MPs were prepared to listen to Puritan grievances. This in turn may suggest sympathy with Puritanism in some form, or it may simply reflect a dislike of the bishops as rivals in provincial affairs. The House of Commons certainly had little or no sympathy for Presbyterianism itself.

As a result of the failure of his parliamentary campaign, Field had come to the inescapable conclusion that the Presbyterian revolution could not be imposed from above. Instead, he turned his efforts to a slower, more secret reform from below, using the style and organisation associated with the continental Calvinist Churches. One pressing need was for a book of discipline. This might provide the basis of a uniform church organisation which, if accepted by the *classes*, could undermine the Ordinal and the Book of Common Prayer. The Presbyterian theorist Walter Travers was largely responsible for such a work, his *Church Discipline* of 1587. But this could only have had a significant effect if a genuine, nationwide framework of *classes* had also existed. As we discovered earlier, it did not. And the efforts of Field and others of a similar mind tended to obscure the fact that there was no general agreement on the exact organisation of a Presbyterian Church. This explains why Travers's book was not uniformly welcomed even by those sympathetic to Presbyterianism.

Nor must it be forgotten that Puritanism itself – Presbyterian or otherwise – was not a nationwide phenomenon. The research of Professor Collinson has revealed that there were whole areas in the country where Puritanism in any form had failed to make a meaningful impact. These areas included the traditional Catholic strongholds of the north, Wales, the West Midlands and parts of the West Country.

5 The Martin Marprelate Tracts of 1588–9

> **KEY ISSUE** Why did the Marprelate tracts fail in their avowed aim of encouraging the spread of Puritanism through criticism of episcopacy?

The next stage in the Puritan campaign created a tremendous storm, but when the dust had settled it was clear that the Puritans themselves had suffered the greatest damage. The *Martin Marprelate* tracts were outrageous, satirical and bitter attacks on the hierarchy of the Church. A rough modern equivalent of the title would be 'Martin bishop-smasher', and the tracts were certainly an exciting read. But they presented a most unsavoury picture of the writer. Were Puritans, then, the violent, sarcastic, offensive, hot-headed, foul-mouthed and destructive individuals as suggested by the style of Martin Marprelate himself? Thomas Cartwright, amongst others, was quick to disassociate himself from the tracts.

So, what damage was done to the Puritan cause by Martin? Firstly, his timing was unfortunate. In the year of the Spanish Armada, when God seemed to have favoured the English and their Church and when unity against a powerful enemy was vital, Martin could easily be accused of being a seditious traitor. Had he forgotten that his Queen was commonly seen as the defender of Protestantism throughout Europe? Secondly, the effectiveness of his secret printing organisation alarmed even those members of the Privy Council who sympathised with the Puritan position.

6 The Puritans Under Attack, 1589–1603

> **KEY ISSUE** Why was Elizabethan Presbyterianism so weak by the end of the reign?

By the end of the 1580s, Puritanism had lost not only John Field, but also its most important patrons. Death had carried away Leicester, Mildmay and Walsingham. In the absence of such defenders, a major and official onslaught against the Puritans was launched: an onslaught which crushed the remnants of Elizabethan

Presbyterianism. Richard Bancroft, chaplain to Sir Christopher Hatton, set the tone with a sermon at Paul's Cross – the open-air pulpit outside St Paul's Cathedral which was used to put across pro-government propaganda. Bancroft explicitly linked Puritans with Separatists and so-called 'sectaries' – such as the much-abused Anabaptists – and gave the whole picture some credibility with a cunningly vague tinge of conspiracy theory. Puritans were allegedly linked to certain powerful men of position and influence. Indeed, government voices were keen to suggest that Puritanism was a vehicle for Presbyterianism, and Presbyterianism a signpost on the road to Separatism. Bancroft was as efficient in uncovering secret organisations as he was at slandering them. A widespread examination of ministers in the winter of 1589–90 laid bare what existed of the Classical movement. Ringleaders were arrested, including Thomas Cartwright. What frightened these men was not so much their appearance before the Court of High Commission as their subsequent examination before the Court in Star Chamber. Star Chamber was the court for traitors. With remarkably bad timing, a few extremist Puritans proclaimed a deranged individual named William Hacket as the new Messiah, and followed up this announcement with another deposing the Queen. For this, Hacket lost his life in July 1591, and Cartwright and his fellow Presbyterians any chance of retrieving their influence and credibility. When they finally emerged from prison, they had little fight left in them. Nor had Elizabethan Presbyterianism.

7 The Separatists

> **KEY ISSUES** What was the nature and strength of Elizabethan Separatism? Why did it have so little impact?

Throughout Elizabeth's reign, Separatists were numerically insignificant. But the government treated them with all possible harshness as potential traitors. The Separatists' denial that church and nation were identical was seen as nothing more than disloyalty under another name.

The most important group of Separatists made its appearance in the 1580s under Robert Browne and Robert Harrison. The group is generally known as the 'Brownists': indeed, the term was used by the government to describe all Separatists. After a spell of imprisonment following the setting up of Separatist congregations in Norwich, Browne left the country and settled in the Netherlands. There, in 1582, he wrote his *Treatise of Reformation without tarrying for any*. The title is revealing, as Browne argued that the Christian should set about reformation without waiting for the permission or guidance of anyone in authority. He further claimed that the Church of England was so corrupt and riddled with papist superstition that the true Christian must shun it at all costs. To distribute works by Browne or Harrison was made a criminal offence for which death was the punishment. In 1583, John Copping and Elias Thacker were hanged for such activities.

By 1584, Browne was back in England, having quarrelled with his Netherlands congregation. He submitted to Whitgift, and was ordained in the Church of England seven years later. But new leaders for the London Separatists were forthcoming in the persons of Henry Barrow and John Greenwood. Barrow and Greenwood were imprisoned for a number of years, but were able to arrange to have several of their works published abroad. In 1593, in the middle of attempting to get a bill against sectaries through Parliament, the government executed the two of them. The title of this measure, passed in the same year, reveals very clearly the link made in the government's mind between refusal to attend divine service in the Church of England and simple disloyalty: 'An Act to retain the Queen's subjects in obedience'. The Act gave the Separatists a number of unpalatable choices. They could either conform or leave the country for good. Should they continue to worship as Separatists, then the death penalty would be invoked.

8 'Anglicanism'

> **KEY ISSUES** What were the fundamental ideas of 'Anglicanism'? How far – at least on a theoretical level – did they represent a challenge to the Elizabethan Church of England?

Of greater long-term significance than the Elizabethan Separatists themselves was a work in defence of the Church of England which was rushed through the presses in time for the debate on the 1593 bill against the 'seditious sectaries'. This was Richard Hooker's *Of the Laws of Ecclesiastical Polity*. It was a monumental defence of the position often called 'Anglicanism'. This is a term which has been avoided in the course of this book so far. It is only right to point out that some historians – and some examiners – use it to describe the Elizabethan Church of England throughout the reign. The present writer prefers to use it to describe a particular theological position rather than the Church as a whole. This permits us to appreciate that there were elements within Hooker's 'Anglicanism' which were deeply disturbing to many of the Church of England's most loyal advocates. In defending his Church against Presbyterians and Separatists, Hooker emphasised the value of tradition and continuity. The Church of England was not, therefore, the result of Henrician, Edwardian or Elizabethan reformation, but a body whose development could be traced from medieval times and beyond. This meant that the Roman Catholic Church of the Middle Ages was indeed part of the True Church – and that the sixteenth-century Church of Rome remained so, despite its errors. This is hardly a position which the likes of Grindal or Whitgift would find comfortable. Significantly, Hooker allotted a relatively minor role to preaching in the scheme of salvation. Using the argument from tradition, Hooker stressed the prime importance of the Eucharist in worship. Worship itself was the most important route to salvation, and preaching was just one of a number of ways for the soul to worship its maker.

What is extraordinary is that, as MacCulloch has pointed out, Hooker's huge work should mention Calvin only nine times. On three of those occasions, Hooker disagreed with him. And full of significance for the future is Hooker's use of the concept of *via media*. This translates as the 'middle way' supposedly trodden by the English Church between the alleged excesses of Calvinist Protestantism on the one hand and the different excesses of Roman Catholicism on the other. Also of great future import was a concept which blends with Hooker's arguments but which was not employed by him. This was the defence of episcopacy as an institution demanded by the law of God (*jure divino*). This case was argued by, among others, Richard Bancroft. The *jure divino* argument is some distance from the viewpoint of Whitgift, who had argued that the Scriptures contained no precise system of government for the Church. Had a specific system been necessary to salvation, then it would have been made crystal clear.

While Hooker largely ignored Calvinism, other writers had the audacity to attack ideas central to Calvinist theology. This, of course, meant attacking much of the theology of the Church of England. In the 1580s and 1590s, some university scholars blended ideas on the importance of sacraments, of tradition and of *jure divino* episcopacy with an attack on the theory of predestination. A major row broke out in Cambridge in 1595 when one of the university chaplains, William Barrett, attacked that theory and, for good measure, Calvin himself. Despite the intervention of influential sympathisers such as the court preacher and Master of Pembroke College Lancelot Andrewes, Barrett's Cambridge career was in ruins. Whitgift himself entered the fray, and drew up the Lambeth Articles of 1595. These restated the centrality of Calvinist theories of salvation to the doctrine of the Church of England. Significantly, the Queen refused to grant these articles official backing on the grounds that Whitgift had been so rash as to pronounce on true doctrine without consulting his Supreme Governor.

The new theology of Anglicanism was to prove nothing short of explosive in the future. When voiced by such men as William Laud, Charles I's Archbishop of Canterbury, it became an important cause of the conflict known as the English Civil War. Its attack on Calvinism, its appeal to the importance of tradition, its lack of emphasis on preaching and its claims for episcopal power would make the position of the 'Conformist' Puritan impossible, and stimulate the very Presbyterianism which Elizabeth had so effectively crushed.

9 Conclusion

> **KEY ISSUES** Why was Puritanism, in theory a considerable threat to the Elizabethan religious settlement, so little threat in practice?

Any attempt to argue that Puritanism was a 'threat' to the Church of England is faced with a number of problems. The first is one of definition. Puritans might or might not be Presbyterians: most were not. They might be Separatist: the vast majority were not. It makes sense to argue that both Presbyterianism and Separatism were, in principle, threats to the Church of England. If the Church of England is to be defined simply as the national Church of the country of England, then only Separatism sought to disband such a system. If 'Church of England' means that system established by Elizabeth in 1559, then Presbyterianism certainly sought to replace the hierarchical and traditional system of church government. The Queen and her ministers assumed that such an attempt would amount to an attack on all aspects of her authority. This assumption meant that the monarch could and did employ formidable powers to suppress that perceived threat. These powers were such that the Presbyterians had little chance of success: therefore, the Presbyterian threat was no real threat at all, despite the noisome gnashing of teeth practised by both sides. Take the case of Parliament and Presbyterian efforts to manipulate it. Elizabeth was able to quash such efforts by voicing disapproval, forbidding the discussion of religious questions and imprisoning the hot-heads. She had further powers – including the proroguing (suspension) or dissolving of Parliament – upon which she never needed to call.

In addition, there is little evidence that Parliament was at all supportive of the Presbyterian position. It threatened too many established interests of the ruling classes, including the right of patronage to church livings. Moreover, Presbyterianism was too much of a leap in the dark to appeal to those whose power rested on stability and social control. And it cut down to size the position of the secular lord, who was a member of a church, and not a ruler of it. All this does not mean that Puritanism in its broader sense was without support amongst the ruling classes. Calls for further reform of the Church and a demand for effective preaching could and did find support in the highest ranks of the government itself. But to identify the House of

Commons with the Puritan interest is mistaken. Puritan voices were listened to with particular attention when MPs felt that the country was under some sort of threat from anti-Protestant elements, be it Catholics at home or Catholics abroad. A reasonably sympathetic MP could rely on the Puritans for some splendid and forthright name-calling: one could enjoy their gift for invective without incurring the wrath of the Queen by actually supporting their demands.

The fact that Elizabeth found herself in conflict with Conformist Puritans was largely of her own doing. Religion was often, in her opinion, a branch of power politics. The interests of evangelising a non-Protestant majority came a poor second to the need for stability and for the safeguarding of her own position and authority. Hence her dislike of prophesyings, her suspicion of mass gatherings to listen to preaching and her own exploitation of church resources. The Grindal episode demonstrates all too clearly where her priorities lay. It also demonstrates the extent to which Puritan attitudes, far from being essentially anti-episcopalian, could be found alive, well and living in the bosom of the Archbishop of Canterbury.

It was, therefore, the Queen's assumptions, priorities and prejudices which dictated the downfall of Grindal and the rise of anti-Puritans such as Whitgift and Bancroft. It follows from this that the conflict between bishops and Conformist Puritans was not inevitable. However, trouble for the future was sown when the anti-Puritans sought a theory upon which to base their opposition to Puritanism. The concept of the bishop as God's chosen instrument was to sever ties between the 'Anglicans' of this persuasion and Puritans – particularly when *jure divino* episcopacy was linked to anti-Calvinist ideas in the reigns of the early Stuart kings.

Historians who argue that Puritans posed a major threat to the Established Church find it difficult to accept that they made a positive and vital contribution towards it. Even though the Puritan minister, pursuing his godly course, might be treated with suspicion by the hierarchy of the Church, his work did much to spread enthusiasm for the Protestant way among those who were not content to sneer and name call, but were, instead, prepared to listen. And Calvinism, it must be remembered, lay at the heart of the doctrine of the Church of England. It is true that Puritans failed to change the organisation and hierarchy of the Church. The Thirty Nine Articles remained, and ministers had to wear surplices and conduct services in the prescribed manner. But what the historian cannot measure is the influence of the Puritan minister in his parish or the Puritan gentleman in his hall: an influence perhaps deeper and more lasting than some of the rituals to which they accommodated themselves.

References

1 P. Collinson, *The Elizabethan Puritan Movement* (Oxford, 1967)
2 D. MacCulloch, *The Later Reformation in England 1547–1603* (London, 1990)

Summary Diagram
Elizabeth and the Puritans

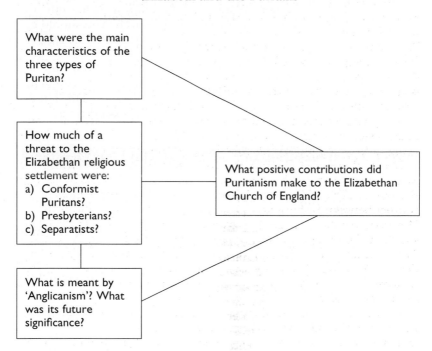

Working on Chapter 3

As you make notes, it will be helpful to bear in mind the aims of the chapter. Puritanism needs definition before it can be assessed, and the chronological approach lets you trace the major themes through your notes. These themes are: how and why did the different types of Puritanism develop? How revolutionary was Puritanism? How did the Queen and the government respond to Puritanism? What effect, if any, did Puritanism have on the Elizabethan Church? You should certainly consider the relative threat posed by the different types of Puritanism. It can help to attempt to give a numerical value to 'relative importance' factors: in this case, a severe threat would merit a score of 9/10 and a minor threat no more than 2 or 3. The actual score matters little: the way in which you justify it does. This kind of exercise generates much debate when tackled in small groups.

Answering structured and essay questions on Chapter 3

It is very possible that examiners might ask questions requiring a comparison of the Catholic and Puritan 'threats' to Elizabeth. Remember to distinguish between the potential threat and the actual threat.

Questions on the Puritans alone follow similar themes. The most straightforward question asks you to comment on the extent of the Puritan challenge to the Elizabethan religious settlement – possibly supplemented by an assessment of how effectively the Queen met the challenge. More demanding are such questions as:

a) How revolutionary was Elizabethan Puritanism?
b) Account for the strength of Elizabethan Puritanism.

You will remember that it is always a good idea to identify keywords in questions, and it is to be hoped that you would give some thought to the meaning of 'revolutionary' in the first question. An answer discussing purely religious change would be inadequate. It is often helpful to rephrase the question before you tackle it. In this case, rephrasing would hopefully allow you to identify the need to discuss the potential political implications of Puritanism: particularly those of Separatism and Presbyterianism.

The second question can be a pitfall for the unwary. Notice that you have to 'account' for the strength of Puritanism. This means that a simple description of how strong the various types of Puritans were fails to answer the question. You need to ask yourself why Puritanism gained the support it did.

It is also possible that you might be set a 'challenging statement' question, asking you to comment on a particular view of Elizabeth's handling of the Puritan issue. One example would be:

c) 'Elizabeth was unnecessarily harsh in her treatment of the Puritans.' How far is this a fair view?

Source-based questions on Chapter 3

Read the Field extracts on p.44–5 and the Grindal extract on p.48. Using both sources and your own knowledge, explain the objections made by Puritans to the Elizabethan Church of England and how far such suggestions represented a threat to that Church. (*20 marks*)

4 Elizabeth and the Catholics

POINTS TO CONSIDER

Chapter 2 demonstrated that the religious settlement of 1559 did not of itself create a fully-functioning new Church. The Church of England at the start of Elizabeth's reign was not a well-equipped vehicle, transporting its admiring passengers towards a future of Protestantism and progress. This chapter examines the historical issues relating to some passengers who would not, one assumes, have cared to travel in a Protestant direction at all. These were the Queen's Catholic subjects.

The chapter will therefore discuss two sets of related questions. First, how did the Elizabethan government deal with Catholicism? To what extent were efforts made to neutralise those who would not conform to the Church of England? If a policy towards the Catholics existed, was that policy consistent throughout the reign? If not, how and why did it change? Second, we need to look at the strength of Catholicism. Is it possible to assess its strength? What evidence can be used, and how valuable is it? What were the various responses of Catholics to the Protestantism of the Church of England? Did those responses change through time? If so, what caused those changes? Bear these questions in mind as you read this chapter for the first time.

KEY DATES

1540 Ignatius Loyola founded the Society of Jesus.
1559 Lords of the Congregation rebelled against regent Mary of Guise.
1568 Mary Stuart fled to England.
William Allen founded the seminary at Douai.
1569 Norfolk/Mary Stuart marriage plot.
Revolt of the northern earls.
1570 Pope Pius V issued Papal Bull *Regnans in Excelsis* excommunicating Elizabeth I.
1571 Ridolfi Plot discovered.
1574 First missionary priests arrived in England from Douai.
1580 First Jesuits (Campion and Parsons) arrived in England.
1581 Act 'to retain the Queen's Majesty's subjects in their due obedience'.
1585 Act 'against Jesuits, seminary priests and other such disobedient persons'.
Parry Plot against Elizabeth.
1586 Babington Plot discovered.
1587 Execution of Mary Stuart.
1588 Defeat of Armada.
1593 Act 'to retain the Queen's subjects in obedience'.
1598 George Blackwell appointed Archpriest.

1 1559–68: The Government Treads with Caution?

> **KEY ISSUES** What principles did the Elizabethan government adopt in imposing the religious settlement on the Catholic majority in this period?

In Chapter 2, it was explained that virtually all the Marian bishops refused to accept the government's legislative changes over matters of doctrine (see page 20). Their deprivation, rather than their execution, resulted. We should remind ourselves that it was not in Elizabeth's interest to pursue an aggressively anti-Catholic policy which would disturb domestic and foreign tranquillity. Equally, it was not in her interests, having adopted a basically Protestant settlement, to grant some form of religious toleration to those who wished to adhere to the old faith. It was an assumption of government that the religion of the country should follow the religion of its prince. Good order required it, and it was an important duty of the monarch to preserve religion. To permit religious division was seen as issuing an invitation to civil war. The question therefore arose, 'What should the government do to ensure religious conformity?' Some things could be done quickly, others required years. First of all, what could be done about the clergy? After all, it was the parish priests who had the responsibility for putting the new service and prayer book into effect. And most of these priests were not, of course, Protestants. As it happened, very few clergy refused the Oath of Supremacy when it was tendered to them in the summer of 1559: perhaps up to 300 in all. We cannot assume that this means that the clergy were fully committed to the doctrine of the Elizabethan settlement. For commitment, however, the Queen was quite prepared to wait. Firstly, it was not possible to replace existing clergy with enthusiastic and trained Protestants. Such men were simply not available in any number. What the Queen could realistically hope for was the longer-term effect on staunch Catholics of attending Church of England services. Habit – doing what your neighbours did – might safely achieve over the years what aggression and punishment might never secure. Indeed, the next generation, baptised, married and buried according to the rites of the Church of England, would hopefully come to regard Catholicism as something un-English and unnatural.

This means, of course, that the Catholic laity was expected to conform outwardly. Under the Act of Uniformity, a shilling fine was levied for each failure to attend church on Sundays and other designated days. This money was intended to be distributed to the poor of the parish where the offence took place. Refusal to take the Oath of Supremacy meant that those holding government offices of any type would lose their positions. A person upholding the Pope as rightful head of the Church – either in writing or speech – lost property for the first offence, all goods and his liberty for the second offence, and was executed for the third. A layman who attempted to persuade any priest to deviate from the order and doctrine of the 1559 Book of Common Prayer was similarly subject to increasing penalties. For, say, persuading a priest to perform a Catholic Mass, the fine was 100 marks (there were three marks in a pound), increasing to 400 marks and then life imprisonment along with forfeiture of goods for second and third offences respectively.

The Act of Uniformity also imposed penalties on clerics who did not follow the required usages of the Book of Common Prayer. In particular, it made it clear that nothing was to be added to the words said in the delivery of Holy Communion. This would therefore prevent the cleric from using the familiar Catholic words to imply the Real Presence of Christ in the bread and wine. In fact, the Act avoided altogether the use of the word 'priest', preferring 'pastor', 'minister' or 'vicar'. This duly underlines the distinction between the Catholic priest and Church of England pastor. Penalty for failure to follow the specified rites – or for attacking those rites – was six months' imprisonment with loss of a year's income in the first instance. A second offence carried one year's imprisonment, and a further offence life imprisonment. Perhaps we should conclude that these penalties were by no means excessively harsh. They would not create martyrs. On the other hand, the fines imposed for attempting to maintain a system of worship outside the Church of England were sufficiently stiff to encourage Catholic gentry to conform outwardly.

However, it would be grossly unhistorical to examine the wording of the Act of Uniformity and assume that its demands were carried out to the letter. A statute may give us some insight into the intentions of the government. Or it may give us insight into what the government wanted people to think its intentions were. What really matters, however, is what happened in practice, and this is particularly difficult to assess. There is evidence from regional studies to show that conservative clergy, whilst operating within the Church of England, nonetheless made it clear that the old ways were the right road to salvation. And the churchwardens who were empowered to impose the shilling fine for non-attendance were often disinclined to do so. Because of this, the fact that there were very few prosecutions in the church courts for persistent absenteeism tells us little. It certainly does not tell us that there was little absenteeism. Nor, of course, should we assume that failure to attend church was a sign of committed Catholicism. A dislike of new ways, a hankering after the 'good old days', a conviction that what was good enough for one's forefathers was good enough for oneself: all these are potent reasons for non-attendance, and none has much to do with theology. The attractions of continuity are obvious. Christopher Haigh (see 'Further Reading'

section on page 152) catalogued problems with clergy who contin
to use Latin, raised the bread and wine as if 'elevating the host', k
the old altar in its traditional position in the east of the Church and
so on.

The cautious policy towards Catholicism should be identified with
the Queen herself. The Protestant members of the political nation, as
represented by Parliament, were much less reluctant to raise the cry
of heresy against Catholicism. At the opening of the Parliament of
1563, Dean Nowell of St Paul's is reported to have said:

> I   The Queen's majesty of her own nature is wholly given to clemency and
>   mercy ... Howbeit those which hitherto will not be reformed, but
>   obstinate ... ought otherwise to be used ... [For] the Scripture tea-
>   cheth us that divers faults ought to be punished by death ... Therefore
> 5   the goodness of the Queen's majesty's clemency may well and ought
>   now therefore to be changed to justice seeing it will not help ... And
>   specially if in anything it touch the Queen's majesty. For such errors of
>   heresy ought not, as well for God's quarrel as the realm's, to be
>   unlooked into. For clemency ought not to be given to the wolves to kill
> 10 and devour, as they do the lambs ... For by the scriptures, murderers,
>   breakers of the holy day, and maintainers of false religion ought to die
>   by the sword.

No doubt the Dean was fairly satisfied by the legislation of this
Parliament. The Oath of Supremacy was to be demanded of a much
wider group. Schoolmasters, lawyers, court officials and MPs were all
required to subscribe. More to the point, a second refusal of the oath
carried the death penalty. Any priest found guilty of saying Mass, and
any laymen who had requested a Mass, were also to suffer death.
Attendance at Mass carried a 100 mark fine. But, once again, we must
not assume that the existence of a law guaranteed its enforcement.
The Queen instructed Archbishop Parker not to demand subscription to the oath a second time if it had been refused the first. This
meant that the death penalty could not be invoked. Nor were there
any executions for the saying of Mass before 1577, when the international climate had changed completely.

2 The Attitude of the Pope

> **KEY ISSUE** Why did the Papacy, in the years up to 1570, not
> condemn the Elizabethan religious settlement?

It might be argued that leniency is the luxury of a monarch who
does not feel under threat. Chapter 2 demonstrated how ruthless
Elizabeth could be in the pursuit or defence of her own interests. For
the first decade of her reign, the Queen felt reasonably secure from

the possibility of a crusade against her on religious grounds by her Catholic fellow monarchs. The friendship – even protection – of Philip II of Spain gave her little reason to make a link between Catholicism among her subjects and the Catholicism of a foreign enemy. Indeed, the Pope himself, for a number of years, carefully avoided a stance opposing Elizabeth. Pius IV may well have anticipated that Elizabethan England might be encouraged to return to the Catholic fold. He even hoped that Elizabeth might send representatives to the Council of Trent in 1559. This Council, first convened in 1545, was intended to spearhead reform in the Catholic Church in the face of the many challenges of the century. What was not immediately obvious was the extent to which it would be under papal control. Previous General Councils of the Church had explicitly challenged papal authority. Elizabeth, it seems, genuinely contemplated sending representatives – until it became clear that the Pope had, by the end of 1560, firmly established his authority over the Council of Trent. Despite the non-appearance of English representatives at the Council, the Pope continued to work constructively for contacts with England. Both he and the Spanish ambassador to England were bitterly disappointed when the Privy Council decided to refuse entry to a papal nuncio (a permanent diplomatic representative) in 1561. It is also significant that the Pope failed to instruct Catholics to shun Church of England services – including Communion – until 1562, and only then in response to a direct inquiry from English Catholics. In fact, English Catholic exiles requested the Council of Trent to excommunicate Elizabeth in 1563. It was a mark of the Pope's increasing frustration that he agreed to do so, and a mark of the desire of Philip II to retain English friendship that he persuaded Pius IV not to carry out his intention at that time.

3 Mary Stuart, Queen of Scots

We have argued that Elizabeth's lenient treatment of English Catholics reflected her view that they represented little threat in the context of a fairly secure international and domestic political climate. If this is an accurate assessment of her motives, it is to be expected that the treatment of her Catholic subjects would have become increasingly harsh as that climate deteriorated from the mid-1560s onwards. Such is indeed the case.

One of the most significant reasons for that deterioration was the flight from Scotland and arrival in England of Mary Stuart, Queen of Scots, in 1568. A full discussion of the Mary Stuart question can be found on pages 129–43. For the moment, it is sufficient to note that Mary had appeared, at various times, to unite in one person all the worst nightmares of English foreign policy: a rival and Catholic contender for Elizabeth's throne and a focus for the traditional anti-

English alliance of Scotland and France. It is at this point that Mary Stuart becomes one of the factors which explain a major change in the Elizabethan government's attitude towards the Catholics. We can use 1568 as a convenient point from which to chart the implications of that change.

4 The Revolt of the Northern Earls, 1569

> **KEY ISSUES** What were the causes of the revolt? Why did the earls fail to win support?

The presence of Mary Stuart in England brought into the open the unresolved problems and dangers facing Elizabeth. The problem which most exercised her Council and Parliament was that of the succession. The Parliament of 1566–7 had insisted that time be allocated for the succession issue to be debated. But this was a matter on which the Queen would brook no interference. In an impressive display of temper, tantrum, threats and abuse, she chose to interpret anxiety about the matter and requests for her to marry as opposition. Mary's arrival reopened the issue. An attractive proposition to one faction at court was a projected marriage between Mary and the greatest of the English nobles, Thomas Howard, Duke of Norfolk. Such a marriage might have the effect of inducing Elizabeth to accept Mary as her heir. This would have two further implications. Firstly, the possibility of a Catholic succession would be materially advanced. The Duke of Norfolk himself might attend Protestant services, but few were unaware that his sympathies were Catholic. Secondly, the marriage could be used as a lever to force out of office the Secretary of State, William Cecil. Cecil's sympathies were most definitely not with the Catholics. In Spain, he saw a power at the head of a conspiracy to destroy Protestantism throughout Europe. In the English Catholics, he saw pawns in the Spanish game. In a Catholic succession to the English throne, he saw the destruction of the Cecils and the triumph of the devil.

The anti-Cecil and 'semi-Catholic' party at Court (to use historian John Guy's term) was backed by certain northern nobles whose Catholicism was whole and entire. The Earl of Northumberland had reconverted to Rome in 1567 and, together with the Earl of Westmorland, had moved beyond the stage of factional intrigue at court into treason. The two earls had been in touch with Rome and with Spain in the hope of obtaining military backing for the cause of Norfolk and Mary. Their only hope of emerging unscathed was to shelter behind the Duke and pray for his success, but Norfolk's plan was brought to a shuddering halt when the Queen heard rumours of the proposed marriage. The royal veto promptly descended, and Norfolk, after the tensest of hesitations, threw himself on the Queen's mercy and his allies to the dogs. He had something of a bumpy land-ing, but got away with a brief spell in the Tower. Westmorland and Northumberland were unlikely to be so lucky. When Elizabeth sum-moned them to court, they came out in rebellion.

Religion, then, provided the justification for the rebellion. Without the Catholic sympathies of the earls, the rebellion makes little sense. After the failure of the rebellion and his subsequent arrest, Northumberland stated that the main aim of the uprising had been to reform religion and to establish and safeguard the position of Mary Stuart as heir to the throne. However, we should add that this reli-gious dissent had been fuelled by increasing isolation from the cen-tres of political power. Both Westmorland and Northumberland had reason to be unhappy about the way they had been treated by Elizabeth. Like all great magnates, they had expected the monarch to listen to their advice and treat with sympathy their petitions for favour. Their expectations had been disappointed, and their disap-pointment was correspondingly bitter. Northumberland felt slighted at not being given some role in the custody of Mary Stuart, and was aggrieved at what he saw as his growing poverty. Both earls were well aware that Elizabeth had sought to weaken their control over the north, where the Crown's authority was traditionally overshadowed by the influence of the great landowners.

As for the rebellion itself, the earls marched on Durham, ejected the Protestant communion table from the cathedral and restored the Catholic Mass. It may be that the intention was to rescue and release Mary from her custody in Tutbury. However, support from the staunch Catholic gentry was not forthcoming. In particular, Lancashire and Cheshire – strongholds of the old faith – failed to join in. The major problem for the rebels was geography. Their power was limited to the North Riding of Yorkshire. To venture towards the centre of government in the south without the prospect of support there would be foolhardy in the extreme. With the approach of a large royal army, Northumberland and Westmorland fled across the border into Scotland.

5 Papal Excommunication, 1570

KEY ISSUES Why did the Pope decide to excommunicate Elizabeth? What were the consequences of that action?

The most significant element in the short-lived rebellion of the north-ern earls was the reaction it called forth from the Pope. On 22 February 1570, to encourage the rebels and to try to whip up support for them from other English Catholics, Pius V issued his Bull *Regnans in Excelsis*. By this, Elizabeth was excommunicated.

1 Pius bishop, servant of the servants of God ... He that reigneth on high,
to whom is given all power in heaven and earth, has committed one holy
Catholic and apostolic Church, outside of which there is no salvation, to
one alone upon earth, namely to Peter, the first of the apostles, and to
5 Peter's successor, the pope of Rome, to be by him governed in fullness
of power ... But the number of the ungodly has so much grown in power
that there is no place left in the world which they have not tried to corrupt with their most wicked doctrines; and among others, Elizabeth, the
pretended queen of England ... has assisted in this ... This very woman,
10 having seized the crown and monstrously usurped the place of supreme
head of the Church in all England ... has once again reduced this same
kingdom ... to a miserable ruin ... she has followed and embraced the
errors of the heretics. She has removed the royal Council, composed of
the nobility of England, and has filled it with obscure men, being heretics
15 ... We, seeing impieties and crimes multiplied one upon another ... do
out of the fullness of our apostolic power declare the foresaid Elizabeth
to be a heretic ... and to have incurred the sentence of excommunication ... And moreover we declare her to be deprived of her pretended
title to the aforesaid crown ... And also declare the nobles, subjects and
20 people of the said realm, and all others who have in any way sworn oaths
to her, to be forever absolved from such an oath and from any duty aris-
ing from lordship, fealty and obedience.

Pius V – who had become Pope in 1566 – was not a man to be governed by considerations of mere politics. When his early hopes for
Elizabeth's conversion evaporated, he began to consider excommunicating her. In March 1569, he had consulted with the Duke of Alva
– Philip II's military commander in the Netherlands – on the possibility of a joint invasion of England by France and Spain. Alva was
unenthusiastic; perhaps, he suggested, the Pope might confer the
kingdom on some Catholic nobleman who would marry Mary. No
doubt Alva was concerned that Mary Stuart ruling alone would mean
an England wedded to Mary's beloved France: a dangerous alliance
indeed for Spain to face. The Pope sent Nicholas Morton, an English
Catholic exile based in Rome, to gauge the reaction of Catholic
nobles to any excommunication of Elizabeth. Morton would seem to
have reported that such a move would be welcomed. Hot on the heels
of this report came news of the rebellion of the northern earls and a
letter from Northumberland and Westmorland asking for papal support. Hence the Bull *Regnans in Excelsis.*

    The Bull was uncompromising. If Catholics continued to obey the
Queen, then they too incurred the sentence of excommunication.
This would deprive them of all the resources of the Catholic Church
in their fight to avoid the pains of hell. If they did obey the Bull, then
this would bring upon them the pains of a traitor's death. *Regnans in
Excelsis* should, therefore, have concentrated the mind of the Catholic
community wonderfully. The time for compromise and evasion had,
it seems, gone for ever. To the historian, an examination of the

impact of the Bull should shed light on some vital issues. How far did Catholics respond to the call for rebellion? What does the episode tell us about their attitude towards papal authority?

As far as the rebellion of the northern earls was concerned, the Bull was an irrelevance. Westmorland and Northumberland had fled before it appeared. What is much more significant is that the Bull was virtually ignored by its intended audience. The English Catholics did not want to know. In fact, since little effort was made to publish and publicise the Bull, they might plausibly have argued that they actually did not know.

This singular lack of response suggests that few English Catholics accepted unconditionally papal claims to fullness of authority over all earthly matters. These claims were not new, and neither was resistance to them. Traditionally, even the most orthodox of Catholic kings of England had expected their subjects to follow them in their attempts to limit papal involvement – or interference, depending on your viewpoint – in anything affecting the power or wealth of the Crown. On top of this was the issue of simple, straightforward loyalty. The landowner of Elizabethan England, Catholic or Protestant, had a very well developed sense of hierarchy and status. This was based on landed property. Rights of inheritance were, he felt, the only protection against the anarchy and upheaval which lay beneath the surface of a violent society. To refuse loyalty to Elizabeth, only surviving child of Henry VIII, was therefore contrary to landowners' instincts for self-preservation. It would be difficult for them to claim the protection of laws of inheritance for themselves and to deny it to the Crown.

Perhaps the most important impact of the papal Bull was the parliamentary legislation intended to neutralise it. The 1571 Treason Acts made it a treasonable offence to deny that Elizabeth was the lawful queen. In addition, it was made clear that anyone using *Regnans in Excelsis* or any other Bull to convert or reconvert a person to Catholicism was guilty of the same offence. However, it is significant that the Queen, once again, refused to allow hard-line anti-Catholics to heap further repressive legislation on to their adversaries. Bishop Sandys's bill to increase penalties for those who refused to attend Church of England services ('recusants') was vetoed by Elizabeth, despite its successful passage through Parliament.

6 The Arrival of the Missionary Priests

> **KEY ISSUE** In what ways did the arrival of missionary priests call into question the government's approach to its Catholic subjects?

Setting aside the perennial problem of Mary and the worries of incidents like the Ridolfi Plot (see page 139), the government had considerable cause for comfort in the immediate aftermath of the excommunication. After all, the signs suggested that Catholics were remaining loyal to the Queen. The rebellion of the northern earls had failed to attract much Catholic support. It is doubtful whether the Bull brought many Catholics who had previously conformed to the Church of England (known as 'church-papists') into open recusancy. Indeed, if the government had felt troubled by such recusants, why release from prison in 1574 a number of important Marian clergy? And so, after the initial flurry when the Bull of excommunication first appeared, Elizabeth's government settled down to its former attitude: Catholicism would wither away with the passing of time. What made its attitude change was a new threat – the arrival in England of missionary priests from continental Europe. These were priests whose aim was to rekindle Catholic ardour and to convert heretics to the true faith.

The missionary priests mainly came from the seminary (or college) of Douai in the Netherlands. Douai was founded by William Allen in 1568. Its aim was to provide a Catholic education for Englishmen and, subsequently, to train priests for missions to England. William Allen had followed a promising academic career at Oxford during the reign of Mary I. He resigned early in Elizabeth's reign on religious grounds and joined other Catholic exiles in Louvain in the Spanish Netherlands, where the university provided a focus and a base for many distinguished English Catholic scholars. The priests trained at Douai were particularly well equipped for the English mission. They were left in no doubt as to the alleged evils of the heretics, but they were also taught to recognise the sinfulness of Catholics past and present which had encouraged the temporary triumph of Protestantism. The priests were able to meet the Protestants on their own ground through in-depth study of the Bible and training in effective preaching. Added to this was the emphasis placed on confession. The confessing of sins to a priest was, of course, a purely Catholic practice, but it had much potential as a vehicle for stiffening the faith of English Catholics who might otherwise have been prepared to conform to the Elizabethan Church. Its importance was that the priest was in a position to transmit God's forgiveness. It is not difficult to imagine the response of an English Catholic who might not have been able to confess for some years. Faced by a priest whose personal holiness was as impressive as his learning, the moment of confession could easily arouse a sense of reborn faith and a commitment to proclaim, rather than to hide, one's faith.

The first four Douai priests arrived in England in 1574. By 1580, about 100 more had come. The impact of these priests – usually referred to as 'secular' priests because they were not members of a particular religious order – is difficult to assess. The problem is that any judgment about their impact depends much upon one's opinion of the state of English Catholicism at the time. Were the missionary priests rescuing the dying embers of a Church, or simply fanning the flame of a slow-burning but still-strong faith? The major historiographical debate on the continuity of Catholicism in England is discussed in detail on pages 79–80.

The response of the government to the Douai priests was initially to press for greater use of existing machinery for identifying and punishing recusants. But sending out such policy directives to sometimes unwilling local representatives of central authority was not the most effective method for dealing with what was seen as a serious threat. In 1577, bishops were instructed to send in a return of the numbers of recusants within their dioceses. In the same year, the missionary priest Cuthbert Mayne was executed under the existing legislation of 1571 for bringing into the country a papal Bull. Two more priests were executed the next year for denying the Royal Supremacy.

7 Missionary Priests and Politics

> **KEY ISSUE** How far could missionary priests be seen as unconcerned with politics?

The death of Mayne gives us insight into an important new theme. Under examination, he had unhesitatingly admitted that he would have supported any Catholic prince who invaded England to restore the Catholic faith. It was small wonder, then, that the members of the Privy Council should be certain that their identification of Catholicism with treason had been confirmed by the activities of the missions. Whether that identification was correct is at least open to debate, despite Mayne's words. It is true, for example, that the missionary priests were instructed not to involve themselves in matters of politics. But it should be remembered that there was automatically a political dimension to any religious activity in late-sixteenth-century England. Whether they liked it or not, the missionary priests were deeply involved in politics. After all, if religious matters were entirely separate from power politics, why was the Pope at this time strenuously seeking to secure an invasion of England? Pius V's successor, Gregory XIII, had followed the standard pattern of papal policy towards Elizabeth. Initial hopes for her conversion were soon dashed, to be replaced by attempts to persuade a generally reluctant King of Spain to sponsor an invasion of England. William Allen himself was invited to Rome in 1576 to advise the Pope on the possibility of an invasion from the Spanish Netherlands under the governor, Don John of Austria. In 1579, another English exile, Nicholas Sander, was encouraged by the Pope to stir up trouble for Elizabeth in Ireland through a small-scale invasion. Sander's tiny force of 80 men was supplemented by the thousand or so Spanish sent by Philip II, but nothing of significance had been achieved by the time the rebellion was over in 1581. It did, however, make still more implausible – or unrealistic – the claim of the new wave of missionary priests in the 1580s that they were uninterested in political matters.

8 The Jesuits

KEY ISSUE What missionary techniques were used by the Jesuits?

This new wave of Catholic missionary activity in England owed much to the impetus provided by English members of the Society of Jesus (Jesuits). It is important to know something of the background to the Jesuits in order to understand their effectiveness as missionaries. The order had been founded by the Spaniard Ignatius Loyola in 1540. Its main purpose was to undertake missionary activity. Loyola had not intended the order as an anti-Protestant weapon, having a much wider concept of its role. This is why Jesuits sought to convert non-Christians in parts of the world where Christianity had previously been unknown. However, as a force to re-awaken loyalty to the Catholic Church, to encourage recusancy, and – crucially – to attract converts from the various forms of Protestantism, the Jesuits were unrivalled. If there was one thing which made the Jesuit priest so effective, it was his use of Loyola's devotional technique known as the *Spiritual Exercises*. This involved meditation on the actual experiences – sensual and emotional – of Jesus himself. Under the guidance of a Jesuit, a layman would often find that such meditation led to a profound outpouring of religious feeling and emotion, which in turn led to a new commitment and a desire to lead as perfect a life as possible. Not all laymen would be able to maintain that commitment. Yet the technique of the *Spiritual Exercises* was a powerful tool, and earned the Jesuits much success, much support and considerable jealousy from fellow workers in the field.

The first Jesuits to arrive in England were Edmund Campion and Robert Parsons (or Persons) in 1580. Parsons set about building up an organisation based on safe houses, which the previous missionary priests had lacked. Wandering individuals without clear destinations in mind were likely to be detected quickly. After all, wandering about was not an acceptable practice in Elizabethan England. Vagrancy laws, deep-set localism and suspicion of foreigners made a stranger without a discernible purpose vulnerable in the extreme. A network of safe houses meant, of course, that the priests had to rely on the gentry class for protection. Even then, detection rates were high.

Parsons's career sheds some light on the major issues affecting the Jesuit mission. Born in 1546, Parsons attended Oxford, but found it a strain to conform to the Elizabethan settlement. Leaving Oxford after some sort of dispute in his college, he decided to study medicine in Padua (Italy). On the way, he stopped in Louvain, and found his Catholic sympathies converted to firm faith through the *Spiritual Exercises*. He was ordained a priest in the Society of Jesus in 1578. Soon after his arrival in England, Parsons attended a clandestine meeting of priests and laymen in Southwark (London), where he read out his instructions. He made it clear that he had been ordered to avoid political matters at all costs. Indeed, the Jesuits, before embarking on the English mission, had obtained from the Pope an interpretation of the Bull of 1570 which allowed Catholics to preserve their allegiance to the Queen until some future date when the times were more suitable for the casting off of that allegiance. However, the Southwark meeting also made it clear that Catholics were not to attend Church of England services under any circumstances whatsoever.

Parsons was fortunate to escape the fate of his companion Campion, who was an effective pamphleteer with a provocative tone of confidence in his faith and in the justice of his position. Campion was captured in a hiding-hole in a Berkshire manor house in the summer of 1581. He was well known to the Queen and members of the government from his Church of England days at Oxford University. He was even offered a senior post in the Church of England if he would turn back to Protestantism. He refused, and was tortured in a vain attempt to extract important information on his contacts. Nor was he humiliated – as intended – in a series of public debates with Protestant theologians, despite being allowed no access to the Scriptures and commentaries by way of preparation. At his trial, he denied that he was anything other than a loyal subject of the Queen. He suffered the traitor's death of hanging, drawing and quartering in December 1581.

9 Parliamentary Response to the Missions

> **KEY ISSUE** What legislation was passed to counter the perceived threat of the missionary priests?

Once again, Members of Parliament came up with bills which demonstrated their concern about a Catholicism which would not fade away in a convenient manner. Once again, it was probably the Queen who moderated their severity. One bill would have made the saying of Mass punishable by death. Another attempted to make the taking of Communion, rather than simple church attendance, the criterion of conformity. This was clearly intended to smoke out those conformists who were really recusants at heart. But the bill which was passed to become the 1581 'Act to retain the Queen's Majesty's subjects in their due obedience' was not quite so harsh, although it was certainly not lenient. Its clauses reveal the extent to which it was a response to the perceived threat of the missionary priests. It opens with an attack on those 'evil affected persons' who had sought to deprive the Queen of the loyalty of her subjects by diverting it to the 'usurped authority of Rome'. The penalty for saying Mass was fixed at a swingeing 200 marks and a year's imprisonment. Anyone who attended Mass was to suffer the same imprisonment and a fine of 100 marks. Penalties for recusancy were substantially increased. Failure to attend church – taking Communion was not required – would carry a fine of £20 per month. To catch those gentry who would claim to attend services in their own chapels within their houses, the Act also required them to attend their parish or similar church four times a year.

However, within three years the Queen had agreed to an Act which recognised the threat posed both by the missionary priests and by the increasing tension abroad. The arrest of Francis Throckmorton in 1583 exposed plans for an invasion of England by French Catholic forces, with Spain and the Pope as the paymasters and Allen and Parsons as the instigators. The assassination of the Protestant leader William of Orange in July 1584 reawoke a fear of a similar fate befalling Elizabeth. On top of this, the Spanish commander, Parma, appeared to be all too close to finally subjugating the Netherlands. What better base than the Netherlands ports for a Spanish invasion? What better preparation than to riddle England with allegedly traitorous priests seeking to turn Her Majesty's subjects from their allegiance? Hence the 1585 Act 'Against Jesuits, seminary priests and such other like disobedient persons'. Any Catholic priest ordained since the beginning of Elizabeth's reign was to leave the country within 40 days. Presence in England thereafter would be high treason. Anyone receiving or protecting such traitors also put themselves in danger of the death penalty. The significance of this Act is that it made things very simple for a government committed to the proposition that militant Catholicism was treason. There was no longer any need to prove that a priest had acted or spoken in a treasonable manner: merely his presence in the country was enough to damn him. According to the historian Philip Hughes, of the 146 Catholics put to death between 1585 and 1603, 123 were indicted (accused and charged) under this Act, rather than under the earlier Acts we have discussed. The Throckmorton and Babington plots of 1585 and 1586 (see pages 140–1) further compromised the reputation of Catholics in general, and further justified the government's stance.

Fortunately for the recusants, the arrival in England of the Jesuits Garnet and Southwell offset some of the long-term effects of the Parry and Babington plots. In particular, Garnet, who quickly became Superior of the English Jesuits, was able to streamline the system of dispatching incoming priests to live with staunch Catholic gentry. These priests might be static, but they would at least be as safe as possible in an unsafe time.

10 The Threat of Invasion from Spain

KEY ISSUE What was the response of the leaders of the missionary priests to the prospect of a Spanish invasion of England?

The period became progressively unsafe as the international situation worsened for Elizabeth. Philip II of Spain was becoming increasingly convinced of the need to invade England. Pope Sixtus V did not like the way Philip II treated the Spanish Catholic Church as if it were his personal property, and needed some convincing that a Spanish invasion of England was a practical possibility. However, he bowed to Spanish requests for financial assistance and, again in response to Philip's demand, made William Allen a cardinal (in 1587). Allen's attitude to the intended onslaught on England is revealing. In his 1584 pamphlet *True, Sincere and Modest Defense of English Catholics ... wherein is declared how unjustly the protestants do charge the English Catholics with treason*, he argued that Catholics – both priests and laymen – continued to be loyal to the Queen despite the Bull of Excommunication. He did not deny that the Pope had the right to depose a monarch, but he pointed out that the Pope had not declared the Bull to be in force. The implication was that the possibility of him so doing was not only hypothetical, but also remote. However, in 1588, with the Spanish fleet (the Armada) ready, Allen prepared *An Admonition to the Nobility and People of England* which was intended to be distributed once the Armada landed in England. Of Elizabeth, he wrote:

1 ... an incestuous bastard, begotten and born in sin ... Fight not, for God's love, fight not, in that quarrel, in which if you die, you are sure to be damned.... Match not yourselves against the Highest: this is the day no doubt of her fall ... Forsake her therefore betime, that you be
5 not inwrapped in her sins, punishment and damnation.

Robert Parsons joined Allen in urging English Catholics to turn against Elizabeth. The call was not heeded. Allen's *Declaration of the sentence and deposition of Elizabeth the usurper* (1588) had urged Catholics to arms to fight on the Spanish side. However, a secular priest named Wright wrote a response which typified the position of the English Catholics. Spain, argued Wright, had launched an attack for political reasons. It was therefore entirely in order for English Catholics to defend their Queen and country against such aggression.

11 Catholic Divisions: Appellants *v* Jesuits

> **KEY ISSUES** Why did divisions arise in the ranks of the missionary priests? What was the effect of those divisions upon English Catholicism?

The issue of loyalty to the Queen was one which created tension within the ranks of English Catholics. The more uncompromising stance of the Jesuits in particular annoyed some laymen and secular priests who, like Wright, were keen to stress practical loyalty to the Queen. More particularly, a sense of rivalry developed between a number of secular priests and the Jesuits. The priests in question maintained a strong attachment to the traditional hierarchical systems of the Church. The Jesuits seemed to cut across such systems. And what was particularly disconcerting was that they were trespassing on the pastoral work of the secular clergy. Most of these seculars felt that the proper place for religious orders was outside the world and inside the cloister. This is symptomatic of the way in which the seculars emphasised the continuity between themselves and the traditional, pre-Reformation Church in England.

The so-called Archpriest Controversy was the fruit of these attitudes. The difficulty arose when it became necessary to appoint someone to assume authority over the English mission. One obvious candidate, William Allen, had died in 1594. It was Robert Parsons whose solution was accepted at Rome. This was to appoint an archpriest, whose task would include some supervision of the secular clergy. In 1598, George Blackwell was appointed to this position. However, some priests found the whole arrangement distasteful. Firstly, it offended the traditionalists as the office of archpriest was entirely novel. Secondly, it was felt that Blackwell was simply a Jesuit appointee, who would naturally favour the Society in each and every action. Blackwell's formal instructions gave some support to this view. They praised the efforts of the Jesuits – and encouraged Blackwell to work closely with them – but ignored the work of the majority of the missionary priests who were, of course, seculars. There is little doubt that some priests were highly antagonistic towards what they saw as an elitist, secretive, arrogant and pro-Spanish organisation.

One group decided to appeal to Rome against the appointment, arguing that Blackwell had, in any case, been appointed merely by the Cardinal Protector of England and not by the Pope himself. Two priests, William Bishop and Robert Charnock, were sent to Rome on the behalf of these objectors. The Pope was out of Rome, and the two found themselves in the hands of Robert Parsons, who made sure they were not given the chance to see the Pope when he returned. They were subjected to what amounted to a trial and thrown out of Rome without a papal audience. This did not prevent the anti-Jesuit

'Appellants' from continuing to appeal to Rome. A bitter pamphlet war between Jesuits and Appellants ensued. One significant contribution came from the Appellant William Watson, who argued that the Queen had been mild and gracious towards Catholics. He also argued that loyalty to the Pope did not include supporting the enemies of England. The Jesuits, he complained, conspicuously failed to display that loyalty. Arguments of this sort pleased the government: indeed, there is evidence that the Appellants were given access to printers who would normally refuse to handle Catholic material. By 1602, the Appellants had won at least part of their case in Rome. Pope Clement VIII instructed the rather arrogant and insensitive Blackwell not to exceed his powers, to take on three of the Appellants as assistants and to refrain from consulting with the Jesuits.

This was not enough for some Appellants. First of all, the Archpriest remained. Secondly – and worse – so did the Jesuits. Thirdly, they hankered after some form of religious toleration from the Queen which would enable a traditional, episcopal hierarchy to be re-introduced. The government was happy to exploit these differences to drive a wedge between the Appellants and the Jesuits, but it was never prepared to allow two religions to coexist within the realm. A Supreme Governor might seek to control one religion for her own ends. Two, and such control was weakened – particularly when one of them upheld the Pope as a rival source of authority. In 1602, a proclamation made it clear that Catholic priests of any type were considered to be threats to that authority. However, those priests prepared to acknowledge their allegiance and submit to the Queen's mercy might expect some (unspecified) favourable treatment. The terms of the proclamation suggest that those submitting in this way would find it difficult to operate as Catholic priests. Perhaps this is why only 13 Appellants chose in 1603 to make a declaration of loyalty. Even then, their declaration stopped well short of an oath of allegiance.

12 The Strength of Catholicism

> **KEY ISSUE** How do interpretations of the impact of the missionary priests differ?

a) Dickens's View

As was suggested in Chapter 1, this issue has generated much debate among historians. A.G. Dickens's elegant and magisterial *The English Reformation*, first published in 1964, established a particular interpretation which has been meaningfully challenged only since 1980. Dickens argued that the Reformation as a whole was neither the product of a rejection of traditional Catholicism at the local level nor an imposed settlement by the monarch, but a combination of the two, fuelled by the ideas of increasingly numerous Protestants. This view has clear implications for his treatment of the Catholics in Elizabeth's reign. It would be difficult for Dickens to argue that there was much continuity between the Catholicism of the pre-Reformation Church and the partly-resurgent religion which he identified with the efforts of the missionary priests. After all, if Catholicism remained strong throughout, the idea of popular anti-Catholicism and support for Protestantism makes little sense. So, Dickens argues for a dying, peripheral faith in the first two decades of Elizabeth's reign, but stresses the importance of the secular and Jesuit priests in reviving something of a corpse.

b) The Revisionists

Christopher Haigh has led the attack by so-called 'revisionist' historians on most elements of the Dickens thesis. Haigh, in *The English Reformation Revised* (1987), argued for a continuity in English Catholicism which was neither severed by the Elizabethan settlement nor in inexorable decline. His evidence came largely from regional studies (such as his own work on Tudor Lancashire) using such sources as visitations made by Elizabethan bishops. In his conclusions, Haigh disagreed with the historian John Bossy, who has argued that Catholicism was more or less dead until saved by the missionary priests. Haigh has made some interesting points about the origins of this 'discontinuity' thesis. He has argued that its first appearance was in the writings of the missionary priests themselves, who would, quite naturally, stress the contribution made by their own orders to the salvation of Catholicism. The temptation would be for these writers to play down the continuity of Catholic worship and the role of the former Marian clergy. This would make the success of the missions more remarkable, and therefore inspire greater devotion among the readers. A good example is the autobiography of John Gerard, a Jesuit who spent 18 years in England. Gerard speaks of his use of the *Spiritual Exercises* on a Catholic gentleman who had just inherited a fine estate from his father.

1   His thoughts were very far from Christian perfection ... As he kept at
    a distance from the seminary priests he was not disturbed by the auth-
    orities ... The persecution at that time [1589] was directed chiefly
    against the seminary priests and on the whole was unconcerned with
5   the old men ordained before Elizabeth came to the throne. It was a dis-
    tinction similar to that made nowadays between secular priests and
    Jesuits, for today the persecution is much fiercer against us ... As I was
    saying, this gentleman lived peacefully with his family on his estate ...
    His eyes were blind to the snares of Satan ... But, in spite of this, he
10 found himself ensnared in the toils of grace. He walked straight into the
    net, was trapped and showed no wish to escape. ... The way, I think,
    to go about making converts in these parts is to bring the gentry over
    first, and then their servants.

Haigh does not wish to deny the importance of the missionary priests. After all, the former Marian clergy were dying out and needed to be replaced. Catholicism could not operate without priests. However, Haigh does feel justified in pointing out that the missionary priests failed to exploit the survivalist Catholicism of the remoter areas of England and Wales, such as the North and West Ridings of Yorkshire, south and west Lancashire, Herefordshire and south Wales. For reasons of proximity to their ports of entry, for the congenial company of people of their own social class, and primarily for reasons of safety, the missionary priests tended to be based in gentry house-holds, more often than not in the south-east of England. This part of England was the prime stronghold of Protestantism. Since the priests were mainly concerned with securing and intensifying the devotion of existing Catholics rather than converting heretics *en masse*, it was an area in which their services were of limited value. Meanwhile, recusancy among the common people of, say, Lancashire or Yorkshire faded due to the inadequate supply of priests. By the end of Elizabeth's reign, the pattern had been set for the future: a future in which Catholicism would become the preserve of a small minority of the upper class until well into the nineteenth century.

13 Problems of Evidence

> **KEY ISSUE** Why does the evidence fail to produce a full picture of the strength of recusancy before and after the arrival of the missionary priests?

There are certain problems in using, as Haigh does, the evidence of regional studies to build up his case that recusancy among Catholics was in being well before the arrival of seminary and Jesuit priests. The first problem is that it is difficult to generalise for the country as a whole from regional studies. Secondly, identifying the precise strength of recusancy is anything but easy – particularly if we are to attempt to date it. Recusants are identified when the government and/or bishops make inquiry. An absence of inquiry does not mean, therefore, no recusants. Indeed, the evidence for assessing the strength of Catholicism – or Protestantism, for that matter – is diffi-cult to handle. A good example of this is the problem of wills. The preamble or introduction to a person's will may reveal his or her reli-gious belief. The bequeath of the soul to Our Lady (Mary, mother of Jesus) and to the saints or company of heaven may be taken to indi-cate a specifically Catholic will, as may references to paying for prayers for the soul after death. Protestant wills would reject any such requests, seeking to emphasise instead the importance of faith as the sole key to salvation. But we need to be aware that the wills were often written by specialists called scriveners who used certain set formulae and wording. It would take a particularly committed person to overcome such bureaucracy as he lay on his deathbed. Similarly, where the clergyman was writing out the will, the pressure on the dying person to conform to the expectations of the clergyman would be enormous.

In trying to back up the complex evidence from wills, the historian is often forced to rely on anecdotal information. This means that the information provided is more by way of an interesting tit-bit rather than an analysis deriving from a major and detailed source. Typical of this is the evidence from law cases in secular and ecclesiastical courts and from the passing comments of letters. Similarly anecdotal is the evidence on the beliefs of those at the bottom of the social ladder: those who were not literate, and whose own voices can seldom be heard. Yet any analysis of the strength of Catholicism should strive to take into account the views of the majority of the population. The anecdotal evidence we do have – persuasively discussed in Keith Thomas's *Religion and the Decline of Magic* – suggests that the Catholicism of the villager had little to do with precise doctrine and more to do with the way in which the Church provided the community with meaningful rituals, such as the 'blessing of the plough'. These semi-magical rites gave a supernatural support to the village in its struggle for survival through the harshness of the working year. The Reformation may well have split the villager from these well-loved ways – by banning them on the grounds that they were pure superstition – without replacing them with anything he could understand. If this picture is correct, then it suggests that any continuity in popular Catholicism throughout the Elizabethan period was not theological or doctrinal. Missionary priests, had they been sent to the areas of Catholic survivalism, would have faced a massive task of education.

It follows from the discussion of the problems of evidence that present conclusions on the strength of Elizabethan Catholicism are bound to be tentative. Haigh makes as convincing a case as possible for the continuity thesis, with the proviso that what continued was, on the popular level, a religion based on community values rather than on a personalised system of salvation. But what is particularly exciting about this area of study is that historians may well be able to re-interpret Elizabethan Catholicism as more research – particularly in the form of regional studies – is done.

14 Conclusion

> **KEY ISSUE** On what grounds might the Queen's policy towards her Catholic subjects be seen as a success?

The Protestant Queen Elizabeth I was bound to see Catholicism as a threat, both to what she genuinely felt to be true religion, and also to her throne. Her Protestant privy councillors felt likewise. That sense of threat was compounded by deteriorating relations with Catholic Spain, by the presence of Mary Stuart and by the Queen's childlessness. It was also compounded by the fact that, in many areas of the country, Protestantism was, at best, unwelcome at the start of the Queen's reign.

By the end of Elizabeth's reign, Catholicism was withering. It was increasingly the preserve of a minority of gentry. Its mass base was dwindling – even in areas remote from the seat of government and Protestant evangelising. From her point of view, the Queen's policies must be judged successful. Apart from the revolt of the northern earls, she faced no major uprising in support of Catholicism. The various plots surrounding Mary Stuart were worrying, but could be used by the government to argue that Catholicism was the religious veneer given to treason.

The Queen must be given credit for refusing to adopt policies of unmitigated harshness towards Catholicism. We have no way of knowing what the effect would have been had Elizabeth allowed her privy councillors and bishops to attempt to stamp out Catholicism with aggressive and punitive legislation from the first days of her reign. It is at least likely that opposition would have been stimulated. Martyrdom is an aid to the persecuted, not to the persecutor. Her religious settlement encouraged conformity through penalties for recusancy which were worth avoiding but by no means excessively harsh: time and usage would cut the ties binding her people to traditional Catholicism.

The threat of Spanish invasion and the activities of the missionary priests forced the Queen into accepting the severe legislation of the 1580s, but she could by this time rely upon her greatest ally: the political and largely instinctive loyalty felt by most Catholic gentry towards their Protestant Queen. The Appellant/Jesuit rivalry was itself stimulated by this issue of political loyalty. The Queen had the good sense not to jeopardise it.

Summary Diagram
Elizabeth and the Catholics

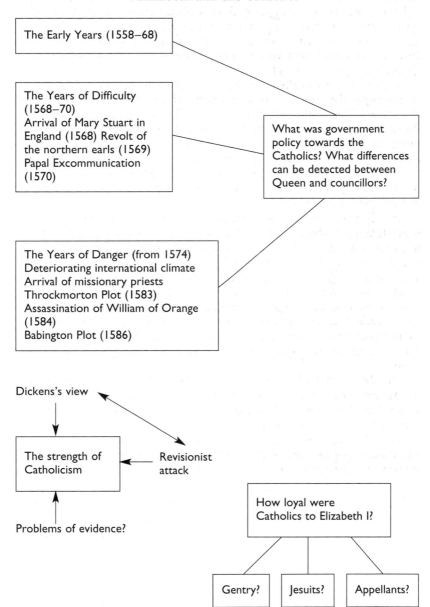

The Early Years (1558–68)

The Years of Difficulty
(1568–70)
Arrival of Mary Stuart in
England (1568) Revolt of
the northern earls (1569)
Papal Excommunication
(1570)

What was government
policy towards the
Catholics? What differences
can be detected between
Queen and councillors?

The Years of Danger (from 1574)
Deteriorating international climate
Arrival of missionary priests
Throckmorton Plot (1583)
Assassination of William of Orange
(1584)
Babington Plot (1586)

Dickens's view

The strength of
Catholicism

Revisionist
attack

Problems of evidence?

How loyal were
Catholics to Elizabeth I?

Gentry?   Jesuits?   Appellants?

Working on Chapter 4

You should target your work on making sure that you are able to offer detailed accounts and explanations of the following:

1. The aims of the Elizabethan government in respect of its Catholic subjects.
2. The methods employed by the government to achieve its ends. Make sure you distinguish between the approaches adopted by the Queen and those advocated by her harsher advisors.
3. An assessment of its success.

Take one large sheet of paper and give yourself the three main headings:

AIMS
METHODS
SUCCESS AND REASONS FOR SUCCESS

The *methods* heading gives you the opportunity to look at policy in the light of the impact of the various crises – Mary Queen of Scots, the revolt of the northern earls, Papal Excommunication, the missionary priests, the threat of Spanish invasion. The level of detail must be sufficient to allow you to prove your contention – which is why the piece of paper is likely to be a very large one. This approach has the additional merit of structuring your work with likely essay questions in mind. You might, however, be wondering about where the discussions of the problematic nature of the evidence might appear. I suggest you include it in the third paragraph as a recognition that assessment of the strength of Catholicism is part of an assessment of the effectiveness of Elizabeth's policies. It is certainly important to know where, why and when Catholicism was strong in England.

Answering structured and essay questions on Chapter 4

It would be very convenient if all examiners came together and agreed that questions on Elizabeth I's religious and foreign policies would follow the chapters of this book. This will not, of course, happen – however desirable it might be. It is therefore a good idea to remember that the wide-ranging question might well require you to use ideas and information from more than one chapter. You might well get a question such as:

1. Did Catholics or Puritans represent the greater threat to the Elizabethan religious settlement? Explain your answer fully.

In this case, you would be using information from Chapters 2, 3 and 4. If you are faced by a question on Elizabeth and the Catholics alone, it will probably ask you to do one of three things:

i) Assess how far Catholics were a threat.
ii) Assess the 'success' of Elizabeth's policy towards the Catholics.
iii) Assess the strength of Catholicism.

Typical questions are:

2. 'Elizabeth's policy towards the Catholics was wise, cautious and by no means over-harsh.' Comment on this view.
3. What were the Queen's aims in tackling the problem of Catholicism? How successful was she?
4. Why and to what extent did Catholicism survive during Elizabeth's reign?
5. To what extent did English Catholics pose a threat to Elizabeth I?

It is a good idea to rearrange these in order of difficulty. Which title is the most difficult? Which is the easiest? Explain your choices.

Many students find 'challenging statement' questions difficult. As has been suggested elsewhere in this book, the best method is to decide on and state your argument clearly in the introduction. This will enable you both to comment on the statement and to clarify the structure of your essay. It would be a good idea to write an introduction for question 2.

Finally, remember that examiners look to reward candidates who show: (a) an awareness of the limitations of the available evidence, (b) a sound grasp of historiography, and (c) a willingness to challenge the assumptions made in the wording of a question. Which questions offer real opportunities to demonstrate these abilities?

Answering source-based questions on Chapter 4

Read the extract from the Bull *Regnans in Excelsis* on p.69 and from Gerard's autobiography on p.79. Using both sources and your own knowledge, explain why, despite the efforts of Pope and missionary priests alike, English Catholicism declined over the period of Elizabeth I's reign.

5 Elizabeth, France and Spain

POINTS TO CONSIDER

You will need to put to one side twenty-first century assumptions about the nature of 'foreign policy' and the way it is conducted. Having done so, bear in mind the following questions as you read the chapter:
What were the foreign policy aims of Elizabeth and her councillors?
Were these aims agreed and consistent?
To what extent did aims change over the reign?
What are the criteria for assessing success in foreign policy?
How far was the policy successful over the period?

KEY DATES

1548 France dispatched 10,000 troops to Scotland. Mary Stuart taken to France.
1557 Under Mary I, England joined Spain in war with France.
1558 Loss of Calais.
Marriage of Mary Stuart and the Dauphin.
Death of Mary I, accession of Elizabeth I.
1559 Treaty of Cateau-Cambrésis.
Death of French king Henry II: accession of Francis II and Mary Stuart.
1560 Treaty of Edinburgh: French troops withdrew from Scotland.
Death of Francis II.
1561 Mary Stuart returned from France.
1562 Treaty of Hampton Court with the Huguenots.
Le Havre occupied by English troops.
Le Havre evacuated.
1564 Treaty of Troyes ended English armed hostilities with France.
1566 Major rebellion against Spain in the Netherlands.
1568 England seized Philip II's Genoese bullion.
1569 Suspension of trade between Spain and England.
1570 Pius V excommunicated Elizabeth I.
1572 William of Orange invaded the Spanish Netherlands.
St Bartholomew's Day massacre.
First stage of the Elizabeth/Alençon marriage negotiations.
1573 Treaty of Nymegen: trade resumed between Spain and England.
1576 Sack of Antwerp.
Pacification of Ghent.
1577 'Perpetual Edict': Spanish army temporarily withdrew from the Netherlands.
1578 Parma's victory at the battle of Gembloux.
1581 Elizabeth provided Anjou with funds to intervene against Spain in the Netherlands.

1584 Assassination of William of Orange.
1585 Treaty of Nonsuch: Elizabeth sent troops under Leicester to the Netherlands.
1588 Defeat of Armada.
1589 Accession of Henry IV of France.
English troops sent to Normandy.
1593 Henry IV converted to Catholicism.
1596 Elizabeth concluded triple alliance with Dutch and French against Spain.
1598 Death of Philip II.

1 Introduction

If the term 'foreign policy' is used nowadays, it conjures up images of cabinet conferences, summit meetings of heads of state, foreign ministers, ambassadors, trade relations, diplomatic staff in a specialised ministry and, if all else fails, war. In the England of Elizabeth, it meant the occasional meeting of the Privy Council, no summits, no foreign ministers, hardly an ambassador in sight, some trade relations, no diplomatic staff and, if all else failed, war.

Most of the essential elements of the foreign policy of a modern state were absent in the sixteenth century.[1] Firstly, the governments of all European countries suffered from a chronic shortage of information about their neighbours. This was partly the result of deficiencies in the organisation of diplomatic life. The exchange of ambassadors was indeed an accepted practice, but few people wanted the position. An ambassador's lot was often not a happy one, and certainly not for an Englishman. England, as a distinctly second-rate nation, could scarcely expect her language to be used in the courts of Europe. So the English ambassador was faced with a language barrier as well as unfamiliar and sometimes distasteful differences in customs, religion, food and climate. The ambassador could not rely on being paid regularly, and might often feel completely isolated. Communications with London meant occasional and long-delayed letters from overworked clerks who were responsible to ministers of state who had internal as well as foreign affairs to handle. Small wonder that Elizabethan ambassadors or envoys were less than perfectly qualified for their tasks. It was frequently a matter of scraping the barrel for someone who was prepared to be poor, isolated, neglected and lonely in unsympathetic surroundings. This no doubt explains the distinctly crass appointment of such unsuitable figures as John Man, a Protestant cleric who was sent to the court of the Catholic King of Spain in Madrid and passed the time making insulting remarks about the Pope. After Man's expulsion, the post remained unfilled. Nor did Philip II of Spain always find ideal candidates for his ambassador to England. After the capable De Silva

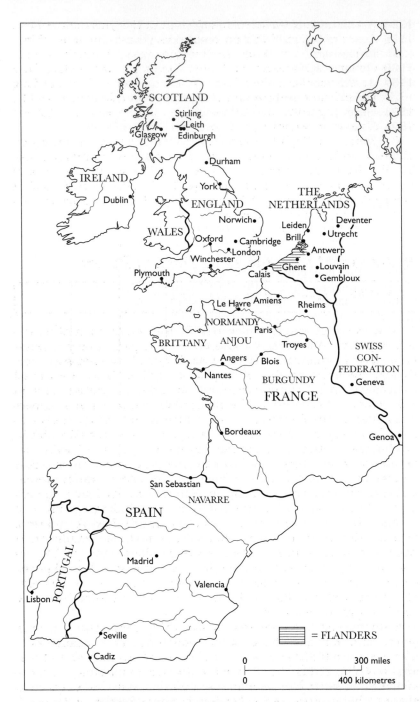

Western Europe c. 1558

requested a transfer from London to Venice in 1568, his replacement, De Spes, set about cultivating a suspicious distaste for most things English. In this, if in nothing else, he enjoyed considerable success. His comments to his master on 'heretic' ministers of state like Cecil are colourful but not the best basis for any policy decisions the King might make. The results of one of De Spes's miscalculations will be discussed on page 102. After his expulsion from England in 1572, the next ambassador, Mendoza, did not arrive until 1578.

Of course, the English government did not have to rely purely on ambassadors for information. Reports from trading organisations like the Merchant Adventurers were of some assistance. But the lack of representatives at the courts of important rulers worked against England's interests. After all, ignorance often leads to suspicion, misunderstanding and bad decisions.

2 Aims and Objectives in Foreign Policy

KEY ISSUE What constituted success and failure?

An assessment of foreign policy must involve a discussion of its success or failure. And success and failure can be judged only in terms of the aims of the policy. But there are frequently problems in establishing what were the aims of a particular policy. Firstly, it is as well to recognise that there existed no blueprint of precise aims in Elizabethan foreign policy. The country was too much of a second-rate power on the European stage – militarily and economically – to have the luxury of undertaking forward-planning in its affairs with its neighbours. This suggests that the only meaningful 'aims' which can be identified are very broad, generalised and common to many periods of history. The first is that the government should prevent the country from being either invaded or controlled by a foreign power. The second is that the government should make sure that relations between states led to a furtherance of English interests. Such interests might be simply economic, or might less simply reflect England's international prestige. However, the second problem is that, although most sixteenth-century monarchs would pay lip-service to the idea of foreign policy being conducted in the best interests of the country, what they really meant was that it should be in the best interests of themselves.

Historians are also interested in identifying consistency, inconsistency, continuity and change within policy-making. If change does take place, the historian needs to know why it happened and who or what was responsible. This interest in the decision-making process – and its development through time – means that it is also necessary to establish the objectives of the decision-makers at the start of the reign.

In addition, there were certain traditional assumptions about other countries – and, indeed, about who should decide foreign policy – which lay behind those early objectives.

3 Assumptions on Foreign Policy

> **KEY ISSUES** How might religious differences affect the traditional alignments in foreign policy? In what ways does the question of Elizabeth's marriage illuminate the importance of councillors in the making of foreign policy?

The most basic assumption at the time was that England's 'natural' enemy was France. It was felt that France would constantly seek to exploit England's troubled relations with Scotland. The objective of English foreign policy would therefore be to curb the French by cultivating the traditional alliance with the Dukes of Burgundy. It was particularly convenient that the House of Burgundy should rule over the 17 Netherlands provinces, because most of the export trade of England – woollen cloth – was sold in the Netherlands' commercial centre of Antwerp. So, a major objective of English policy was that the Netherlands should retain their traditional independence. This was based upon the looseness of the links between the provinces and their strong sense of separate identity – factors which would work against the Netherlands being assimilated into the great monarchies of France or Spain. However, for Elizabeth, the situation was complicated by the fact that the Burgundian ruler of the Netherlands was none other than the King of Spain. It was undeniably awkward that Philip was a devout Catholic and that Elizabeth had established a markedly Protestant regime. However, Philip had, it seemed, every desire to keep the traditional Anglo-Burgundian alliance for the same reasons as Elizabeth: it was a bulwark against French ambitions. But what if Philip should turn against England, using the Netherlands both as an economic weapon and as a convenient springboard for the invasion of a heretical kingdom? And what if the worst possible happened: a Catholic alliance between Spain and France against England, with the Netherlands the key to English defeat? After all, England was the most powerful Protestant power in Europe. It is scarcely surprising that Spain and France should increasingly see Elizabeth as the centre of an international Protestant conspiracy. It is even less surprising that English Protestants should similarly see growing links between Spain and France as evidence of a Catholic alliance aimed at smashing heresy once and for all throughout Europe. This theory was held most firmly by those of Puritan sympathy. There is evidence that, as the 1570s progressed, an increasing number of Elizabeth's councillors sought to discard completely the old ideas about Anglo-Burgundian alliances in favour of a very new objective: a Protestant alliance system to counter the supposed Catholic threat. The reasons for this major transformation will be discussed fully on pages 96–7.

One assumption remained valid throughout the reign, and nowhere more so than in the mind of Elizabeth: the special right or prerogative of the monarch to decide foreign policy. Councillors offered advice, and that was all. This kind of blunt statement of principle may, however, be misleading. Although councillors were frequently in disagreement, they expected the monarch to be at least responsive to their advice and show that she valued their views. After all, some advice was offered from deep personal conviction, some from the feeling that the safety of the country was at stake and some from the selfish but no less important motives of personal status and profit. It would have been politically unwise for Elizabeth to have made arbitrary decisions which took no account of the opinions of influential and wealthy men.

The issue of Elizabeth's possible marriage provides some insight into both the limitations and the reality of the influence of the councillor.[2] Marriage, in fact, was an important weapon in the foreign policy armoury. One problem with this weapon was that it could generally be fired only once. The usual assumption, however, was that firing was necessary. Elizabeth's talk about the virtues of the unmarried state was, at the start of the reign, taken by her councillors as maidenly but impractical in political terms. The most serious candidate in 1559 was probably the Archduke Charles, younger son of the Austrian branch of the Habsburgs. A match between Elizabeth and Charles was one way of keeping Philip II both happy and a potential ally against French aggression in Scotland. It had, therefore, been recommended by those in the Council such as Arundel who opposed direct English intervention in the affairs of her northern neighbour. This proposed match came to nothing, in part because the opinion of the Council was not unanimously in favour, but mainly because Elizabeth had a favourite candidate of her own. This was the home-grown Robert Dudley (Earl of Leicester from 1564), inconveniently married and then conveniently widowed in the autumn of 1560: but not so conveniently as to scotch all sinister rumours surrounding the death – by a fall – of his ailing wife. His main problem, however, was that he lacked meaningful support in the Queen's Council, and that Cecil and others saw him as a catastrophic candidate: a man tarnished by the unsavoury rumours of his wife's fate. At what point the Queen reluctantly decided to forego the marriage with Dudley is not clear. What is clear is that her councillors' opposition did lead her to act against her own desires. Nevertheless, Dudley retained a place in her affections which made him uniquely influential. And with the failure of his marriage plans came a commitment to an aggressive Protestantism which had vital implications for the conduct of foreign policy in the future.

To assess the foreign policy of Elizabeth, the reader will need to bear in mind the criteria for assessment as outlined in the preceding paragraphs: particularly the need to distinguish between aims, objectives and assumptions and to be prepared to account for continuity and development. To make the topic as a whole more manageable, this chapter will, after an analysis of the first years of the reign, consider the relations between England and France and England and Spain separately. To assist with the analysis of the way in which foreign policy developed, the sections of the chapter are divided chronologically.

4 Foreign Affairs in the First Years of the Reign (1558–9)

KEY ISSUE In what ways did religion impact on events in this period?

In Chapter 1, it was made clear that Elizabeth inherited a realm at war with France. It was also explained that the loss of the sole English territory in France – Calais – had been humiliating for the Marian government. This loss had, it seemed, exposed the dangers of yoking English foreign policy to the needs of Spain. The same chapter discussed the peace negotiations between England, France and Spain that took place at Cateau-Cambrésis: negotiations in which England's position was not strong. In particular, there was the danger that France might question the legitimacy of Elizabeth's title to the throne. Might not a rival claim be made on the behalf of the Catholic Mary Stuart, Queen of Scotland and wife of Francis, heir to the French throne (see pages 132–3)? As it happened, Henry II of France was much less interested in trying to put his daughter-in-law on the throne of England than he was in securing peace. This did not mean that the French were prepared to return Calais, but it did mean that they were prepared to let the English save face somewhat. Hence, it was agreed that Calais would be held by the French for eight years. After that period, England would either get it back – which was, in practice, highly unlikely – or receive some monetary compensation for its loss, which was only marginally more likely. The probability was that England would receive neither the town nor the compensation. Such proved to be the case. The signing of the treaty was a relief to the English, but what appeared to be an ominous friendship developing between France and Spain following Cateau-Cambrésis was not. Might this not be the start of the anticipated Catholic conspiracy against Protestantism throughout Europe? If so, the old assumptions about France and Burgundy would be frighteningly irrelevant. However, such fears were somewhat lessened by the apparent willingness of the King of Spain to seek and retain England's friendship in the time-honoured manner. Historians traditionally point out that Philip II saw himself as a candidate for the marriage it was assumed Elizabeth must soon make and that he had no desire to see the Guise dynasty use Mary Stuart to control not only Scotland and France, but England as well. On the other hand, recent research by Parker suggests that the king's letters reveal a deep anxiety about the religious direction England appeared to be taking and even a desire to launch an invasion if only his finances would permit. They did not. In any case, Philip found himself facing a decade in which the menace of Turkey loomed larger than the heresy of Elizabeth.

Philip's attitude was fortunate for England because 1559 saw two events of great importance in the development of, and tensions within, the country's foreign policy. The first was the rising of the Protestant Lords of the Congregation against Mary of Guise, the Catholic regent in Scotland. Here was temptation indeed for England to intervene militarily in Scottish affairs. If English forces were able to contribute towards a successful Protestant rebellion, then the danger of Scotland being used as a base for French attacks on England would recede. If French troops could be prised out, then the Guises would lose one of the most important weapons in their armoury. It was, in fact, very important for England to see the power of the Guises curbed. This was because the second event of great significance was the death of Henry II and the succession of the young Francis II to the throne of France. The new French royal couple were soon using the English royal arms along with those of France and Scotland: a particularly clear reminder of the potential dangers posed by Mary Stuart to the security of Elizabeth herself. These two developments were grist to the mill of those who saw foreign policy as a battleground between Protestantism and Catholicism. But Elizabeth's Council was unlikely to speak with one voice on this, or any other, issue. In particular, the remaining members of Mary I's Council, such as Arundel, Winchester and Petre, were opposed to risky intervention in the affairs of other states in the interests of national and international Protestantism. The main supporter of such intervention was the Queen's Secretary, William Cecil. Cecil wanted military support for the Scots and, exploiting fear of the Guises and Elizabeth's fury over the French claims to her title, he eventually had his way. Details of what turned out to be a most gratifying success story for Elizabeth are provided in Chapter 6. In short, the use of English sea and land power brought the French forces in Scotland to the negotiating table. By the Treaty of Edinburgh (1560), both French and English troops withdrew from Scotland. Traditional assumptions and equally traditional objectives were, it seemed, vindicated by this success. France had indeed proved to be the greatest threat, and that threat had been successfully – if temporarily – thwarted by resolute intervention in Scotland.

It is important to look carefully at Cecil's approach to Scottish intervention, since it provides insight into a number of Elizabeth's attitudes which themselves had major implications for the conduct of foreign policy. Cecil was well aware of the need to take into account his Queen's near obsession with the rights of legitimate sovereigns. Support for the Scots nobles was not to be treated as an opportunity for depriving Mary Stuart of her title as Queen of Scots, however many times she chose to sit under canopies bearing the royal arms of England. Cecil was also careful to play down the fact that the Queen would be aiding those whose Protestantism was considerably more radical and Calvinist than her own. He was aware that Elizabeth was unlikely to conduct foreign policy with the interests of Protestant solidarity at or near the forefront of her mind. Her opinion was that such interests led, all too frequently, to rebellion against legitimate authority. The mantle of Protestant champion sat uneasily on her shoulders.

5 Relations with France, 1562–83

> **KEY ISSUES** What did the failure of English intervention in France (up to the Peace of Troyes, 1564) reveal about the different emphases within English policy? What was the significance of the Treaty of Blois? What does the English response to the Massacre of St Bartholomew's Day reveal about the contrasting aims of Queen and Council? What does the Anjou episode reveal about the nature of English foreign policy?

If ever the Queen needed an object lesson in the dangers of religious division – and she did not – she need have looked no further than France. The conflict between the Calvinist Huguenots and the Catholics was intensified at the accession of Francis II in 1559. This was because the Guise faction used its influence over the young king to urge him to a zealous persecution of the Protestants: partly to defend Catholicism and partly to defend the Guises against such important Huguenot nobles as the Prince of Condé. The resulting unrest – the so-called Tumult of Amboise – worked against the Guises and enabled Catherine de Medici, the mother of the ailing king and an enemy of the Guise faction, to persuade Francis to relax the heresy laws pending the discovery of some formula for easing the religious strife. When Francis died in December 1560, Catherine was in a sufficiently strong position to oust the Guises from their predominance and to assume the role of regent to her ten-year-old son, Charles IX. In his name, she issued an edict which recognised the principle of peaceful religious coexistence. But she underestimated the extent of the hatred between Catholics and Huguenots. By the autumn of 1561, the Duke of Guise had withdrawn from court and was rapidly building up an alliance to defend Catholic interests. Significantly, he sought and obtained financial and other help from Philip of Spain who saw in the crisis a splendid opportunity both to defend his faith and to exploit divisions within France.

In England, the renewed conflict, and a massacre of Huguenots at Vassy by the Duke of Guise, provided exactly the same opportunities except, of course, it was the Protestant religion that was to be defended. With a successful Scottish adventure behind them, there was less hesitation about a military intervention in France. Even the Queen, whose hesitations were becoming a factor to reckon with in any policy, was keen to contemplate such a step. This is not to say that the motives of all concerned were identical. The most enthusiastic interventionist was Sir Robert Dudley (soon to be created Earl of Leicester). His reasons were by no means purely religious. He did not need to prove that he was the Queen's favourite – everyone knew that he was – but he did need to prove that he was a force to reckon with in matters of high policy.

What interested the Queen as much as thwarting the Guises was the chance of recovering Calais. The Huguenots might be persuaded to hand over Calais as the price for successful English assistance.

By the Treaty of Hampton Court (September 1562), Elizabeth promised loans and military aid to the Huguenots. But the English troops – under the command of Dudley's brother, the Earl of Warwick – were as much victims of the incompatible objectives of the government as they were of the successes of the Catholic forces. Having seized Le Havre as a base, the English were soon destroying Protestant solidarity by trying to exchange Le Havre for Calais. This was hardly likely to impress the Huguenots, who had patched up some sort of reconciliation with Catherine de Medici. Huguenot and Catholic combined to expel the English from French soil. Plague in Le Havre and the prospect of the combined French attack resulted in the surrender of the town in June 1563. The Peace of Troyes in 1564 ended armed hostilities with France: a hostility which had, in any case, been lessened with the death of Guise and the studied friendliness of Catherine de Medici both towards Elizabeth and towards the Huguenots themselves.

This intervention in France usefully reveals the lack of definite and agreed objectives in English foreign policy at this stage. The religious motives of Dudley – fed by his desire for status at court – must be set against the willingness of the government to jeopardise the Huguenot cause by seeking to claw back Calais. As for Elizabeth, the episode had strengthened her dislike of assisting rebels against a legitimate monarch and had done nothing to encourage her fellow-feeling for continental Protestantism. Dudley and others continued to press for support for their co-religionists, but, as the years went by, Elizabeth's inability to come to firm decisions blended with her distaste for rebellion. Those who wished for a precise and Protestant foreign policy were baulked by the Queen.

There are two main elements in Elizabeth's policy towards France from 1564. These elements are linked. The first stemmed from the deterioration of relations with Spain as the decade drew to an end. This meant that the traditional anti-French assumptions might have to be amended in the interests of securing potential allies against Philip II. The second element was the threat from the Guises, whose aggressive Catholicism might lead them into the very alliance with Spain that Cecil so gloomily contemplated. This does not mean that Elizabeth and her councillors came up with some master-plan to counter a future threat: instead, English foreign policy is best seen as a set of responses to various crises. The diplomatic crisis and suspension of trade between Spain and England (see pages 101–3) in 1569 prompted Elizabeth to enter into a round of marriage negotiations with Henry, Duke of Anjou – second son of Catherine de Medici – between 1570 and 1571. It was, of course, convenient that Catherine was the bitter enemy of the Guise faction. Elizabeth had no intention of marrying Anjou, but the discussions were nearly as good as a treaty of friendship. In fact, as Anjou faded from the scene, Catherine's youngest son, Francis, Duke of Alençon, was wheeled on stage to take his place: but it was the Treaty of Blois of 1572 which was the significant result of this friendliness. By the terms of this treaty, France in effect abandoned the claims of Mary Stuart to the throne of England. The two countries established a defensive league which was intended to prevent the possibility of Spanish aggression against either.

On 24 August 1572 came an event which put this fragile alliance with France to the most demanding of tests: the Massacre of St Bartholomew's Day. The massacre had followed from a bungled attempt by Catherine to remove – that is, murder – the Protestant leader Coligny, who was, in her view, becoming dangerously close to her son Charles IX and thus about to embroil the French in a disastrous religious war with Spain. Coligny was killed at the second attempt, but the Paris mob turned the affair into mass murder. At least 3000 Huguenots died in Paris alone. Protestant England was understandably horrified. Might not Elizabeth herself be the next victim? What would be the fate of English Protestants if Mary Stuart were to succeed to the throne? Small wonder that the militant Protestants of the Queen's Council exerted every effort to persuade her to send an army to the defence of the Huguenots, her religion and her throne. Elizabeth, however, was largely unimpressed by the clamour. Protestant the Huguenots might be, but they were, in her eyes, also rebels against a legitimate monarch. In any case, had she not witnessed the disasters of her previous campaigns on their behalf? Was it sensible to throw away the tentative and newly-established friendship with Catherine de Medici for the sake of such a cause?

What the English actually did was to negotiate with both sides. Unofficially, help was offered to the Huguenots, and yet talks were renewed with Catherine de Medici on the Alençon marriage. It is unfair to label the English response as confused. In all probability, it was Elizabeth who prevented the country from launching into a gravely hazardous military adventure. It was hazardous because England lacked the resources to maintain a campaign against the French Crown, and because further interference in France in the defence of Protestantism would cement the links between Spain and the Guises. It might result in the conflict being turned into a Europe-wide religious war, with untold consequences. The English response might not have been heroic, but it made sense.

There were other reasons for not losing sight of the Alençon marriage (which should at this point be referred to as the Anjou marriage – the suitor was the same, but his title had changed when his elder brother inherited the French throne in 1574). Firstly, the fate of the Netherlands – that most abiding concern of the English – was once more in the balance. The Spanish commander, the Duke of Parma, had been particularly successful against the rebel forces in 1578 (see page 104). Secondly, it looked as if Anjou intended to play a signifi-cant part in the Netherlands struggle. Catholic though he was, Anjou was fiercely anti-Spanish. To the increasingly desperate rebels of the Netherlands, Anjou looked a better source of help than the hesitant and often unsympathetic Queen of England. But, for Elizabeth, the danger was that Anjou would simply replace Spanish authority over the Netherlands – which was at least hedged about by frequent Spanish inefficiency and permanent Spanish communications prob-lems – with French authority. One way to neutralise Anjou would be to outbid him by offering firm commitment in the shape of money and troops to the rebellious provinces. This policy was, of course, much favoured by the more zealous Protestants of Elizabeth's Council. But the Queen's habitual dislike of rebels was unchanged: she preferred to play the marriage card yet again. The difference this time was that Elizabeth was genuinely prepared to marry Anjou. This was partly for emotional reasons. At the age of 46, Elizabeth's days of playing the enjoyable and ego-boosting game of courtship were fast drawing to an end. Faced with the prospect of marriage into one of the greatest royal families, she discovered that she wanted marriage – badly. There were also cogent political reasons for marrying Anjou. As his wife, Elizabeth could hope to control his behaviour in the Netherlands, whilst at the same time using him as a threat to persuade the Spanish to negotiate a settlement with the Netherlands provinces along the lines of the Pacification of Ghent (see page 104). This would, at the very least, free the provinces of Spanish troops.

Elizabeth faced both political and emotional opposition, not only from members of the Council but also, it would seem, from public opinion. This determined opposition was based in part on the fear that England would thereby be controlled by France in the French interest, and in part on anti-Catholic feeling. It is hard to escape the conclusion that Elizabeth became a victim of her own propaganda.

How could the Virgin Queen, protectress of Protestantism, nursing mother and Supreme Governor of the English Church, so tarnish herself? Elizabeth gave way: there was no marriage and, in August 1581, she settled for providing Anjou with funds for intervention in the Netherlands. To use a Catholic in the defence of the provinces demonstrates very clearly that the Queen's aims and objectives were entirely traditional, even if her means were not. Rather than seek to defend and spread Protestantism – which would have been an entirely new aim for English foreign policy – she sought to maintain the Netherlands' semi-independence in the interests of England's security alone. Unfortunately for her, Anjou's expedition was a disaster. By 1583, he was back in France and, the next year, dead.

The Anjou episode provides a number of helpful insights into the nature of Elizabethan foreign policy. It serves as a reminder of the centrality of the Netherlands to English concerns. It demonstrates the potential role of marriage in foreign affairs. It also demonstrates the fact that Elizabeth was willing and able to reject the advice of those who demanded a military intervention in the Netherlands for religious reasons. But this does not mean that Elizabeth was able to ignore concerted and virtually unanimous demands which, in theory, infringed her prerogative over foreign affairs. For the second time, she allowed herself to be persuaded out of a marriage.

6 France, 1584–1603

KEY ISSUE Why was English support offered to Henry IV?

The death of Anjou was not without significance for Elizabeth's wider interests. Anjou's brother Henry III was childless, and there was a real prospect of the Huguenot, Henry of Navarre, succeeding to the throne of France. But this, the Guise faction could not stomach. From Elizabeth's point of view, danger lay in the alliance between the French Catholic League – dominated by the Guises – and Philip II. Under the Treaty of Joinville (1584), the King of Spain was subsidising the League, partly in the hope that, if it succeeded in crushing Navarre and the Huguenots once and for all, Philip need not fear French intervention against his forces in the Netherlands. In addition, the League was particularly strong in northern France. This might make the channel ports of France available to Spain for an invasion of England: an invasion which was itself part of Philip's Netherlands strategy (see pages 106–7). By September 1589, Philip had decided to give the League support in the form of Spanish troops. The Duke of Parma was ordered to move Spanish forces in the Netherlands to the French frontier.

Both the Duke of Guise and Henry III had been victims of assassins by mid-1589, but, even though Henry of Navarre was crowned as Henry IV, the situation was still perilous from the English perspective. The alliance between the League and Philip II was simply strengthened by this setback, and Elizabeth was faced with urgent demands for assistance from Henry IV. She had little choice but to commit herself to sending both money and troops in the autumn of 1589. But by 1590, Spanish troops were in Brittany. If Spain overran Normandy, then Spanish-controlled Brittany could link up with the Spanish army in Flanders. This is why Elizabeth constantly complained of Henry IV's lack of interest in dealing with the problem of Normandy. Henry himself was under no illusions: Elizabeth was, as always, responding to English interests and not to those of international Protestantism. Nor did Elizabeth call off her support when Henry IV converted to Catholicism in 1593. In fact, this decision was politically helpful from the English point of view. Conversion gave Henry the opportunity to unite France. His decision not only pleased the Catholic majority, but also made the Catholic League irrelevant. He also offered toleration to Huguenots. France might therefore become once again an effective counterbalance to Spain. Henry was hardly likely to form a friendship with Philip II, and his debts to the Queen meant that a convenient Anglo-French hostility towards Spain could be maintained. English troops were withdrawn from France by 1595, leaving Henry to unite the country by the traditional method of focusing attention on a common and foreign enemy. Only when Henry's national war with Spain started to go badly were English troops sent back (in 1596). As part of her attempt to shore up Henry IV, Elizabeth concluded a triple alliance with the Dutch and France in 1596 and, as part of the alliance, was obliged to recognise the United Provinces as a sovereign state. It was typical of Elizabeth's obsession with the rights of legitimate rulers that she should have been so reluctant for so long to give official sanction to the rights of rebels.

In 1598, Henry IV made a separate peace with Spain which simply accepted the territorial position laid out at Cateau-Cambrésis so many years and so many lives before. The need for English troops in France was at an end.

7 Relations with France: A Conclusion

> **KEY ISSUES** What changes had taken place in English attitudes towards France over the period of Elizabeth's reign? What do relations with France demonstrate about conflict between the Queen and some of her councillors over foreign policy aims? To what extent can success be seen as more the result of fortune than of English actions?

In section two, it was made clear that an assessment of foreign policy demands a precise set of criteria. It was suggested that the historian is interested in continuity and change, and that it is therefore necessary to identify the assumptions made by the decision-makers at the start of the reign to permit the tracing of developments in foreign policy objectives. The most important change, of course, was in the old assumption about France being the 'natural' enemy. Spain became identified as the greater threat to English interests – in the shape of the Netherlands – and to the security and safety of England itself. The attempt to curb Spanish dominance over the Netherlands might have been a new objective, but the old fear of French control of the self-same provinces was difficult to shake off.

Indeed, the formation of new objectives in English foreign policy was not easy because the aims and objectives of Elizabeth and her councillors were not always identical. There were those who wished to make Elizabeth the saviour of international Protestantism. This new aim, Elizabeth successfully resisted: partly due to her realistic appraisal of English weakness, and partly due to her inability or unwillingness to depart from the assumption she never shed – that the encouragement of rebellion was the unacceptable face of foreign policy. Given the Queen's chronic indecisiveness, it is hardly surprising that she was unable to commit herself to radically new aims and objectives except when those were imposed upon her by circumstance. For example, the decision to send troops to France in 1596 was hardly a decision at all: it was a response to events beyond Elizabeth's control.

Generally speaking, when there were policy decisions to make, it was the Queen who made them. Her councillors might feel frustrated or beside themselves with exasperation, but her right to make those decisions was all but unchallenged. As we have seen, Elizabeth gave way only when her use of the dangerous weapon of marriage was widely deplored.

How, then, to assess the success or failure of English foreign policy towards France? The broad aims of the government were achieved in the sense that the country had not been invaded or grossly manipulated by France. The objective of preventing the Guise faction from using the French monarchy, the French Catholic League and/or alliance with Spain to subvert Elizabeth was indeed achieved. But it cannot be argued that English policy was responsible for this. English military intervention was less than successful, and the eventual neutralising of the Guises owed more to French internal and external politics and the assassin's knife than it did to English interference.

In the introduction to this chapter, it was noted that the foreign policy of English monarchs had been geared towards the satisfying of personal ambition. The aim had often been prestige or, better still, glory: sometimes, it had been dynastic ambition or simple greed for territory. War, of course, was the most convenient means; France, the arena and England, the arsenal. But Elizabeth I, it seems, had little interest in winning fame this way. The closest she came was her lust to regain Calais. Her failure was unsurprising, but it hurt nonetheless.

8 England and Spain, 1560–74

> **KEY ISSUES** Why did relations with Spain deteriorate over the
> period? What examples can be found of Elizabeth reacting
> pragmatically to events?

Relations between England and Spain in the early 1560s were less
than open and cordial. Given the religious differences, this is hardly
surprising. But joint suspicion of the Guises was sufficient to keep the
two powers reasonably friendly. This explains why Philip II was keen
at this time to dissuade the Pope from excommunicating Elizabeth as
a heretic. Better a Protestant Tudor Queen of England than a
Catholic Stuart Queen when the latter was a tool of the Guises.

Potential for serious conflict between Spain and England lay in the
importance of the Netherlands to the well-being of the latter (see
page 90). In 1566, Philip II faced a major rebellion in the
Netherlands. Significantly, the immediate cause was resentment at
the Spanish King's attempt to run the Netherlands like a colony of
Spain. Spanish officials, it seems, were undermining the traditional
importance of the great nobles at the Council of State, which was the
policy-making body in the provinces. If this attempted centralisation
seemed sinister to the nobility and the town authorities, it also
seemed sinister to England, especially when Philip sent a Spanish
army under the Duke of Alva to suppress the rebellion (1567).
Spanish troops, Netherlands' ports, and a military commander with
an impressive reputation and a remit to destroy heresy: here was a
prospect to worry the calmest of Elizabeth's councillors.

It is not possible to construct a convincing argument that Elizabeth
followed a consistent policy towards the Netherlands in the following
decades of turmoil. There are certainly many instances where
England's policy seemed to be nothing more than a reaction to circumstance. However, one must take account of the basic assumptions
which underpinned Elizabeth's responses. In the introduction to this
chapter, it was argued that it suited England to see Spanish authority
over the Netherlands maintained in preference to that of France. But
it was important that this authority was not backed by an army of occupation, which would effectively destroy the traditional semi-independence of the Netherlands. Nevertheless, the English had to
recognise the fact that, although they might seek to influence events
in the Netherlands, they were in no position to direct them. This,
Elizabeth was realistic enough to acknowledge. Not all her councillors
were so clear-headed.

By 1568, the rebels in the provinces had suffered major setbacks.
Two of their leaders, Horn and Egmont, had been executed. Others,
including the powerful William of Orange, had been defeated in
battle by Alva. Elizabeth was not prepared to commit English forces to

the rebel cause, partly due to that distaste for rebellion which has featured so regularly in this chapter, and partly because England lacked the military muscle to face a commander such as Alva in open battle. Elizabeth had learned from the disasters of 1563–4 in France (see page 95)) that sending a small expeditionary force in theory to help a just rebellion, but in practice to further her own interests, was unlikely to end in success. So, a policy of harassment seemed wise. It was potentially damaging to Spain, it might be possible to dissociate the English government from it if necessary, and it might even yield a profit.

Certainly there were members of Elizabeth's Council who saw a splendid opportunity to strike a blow at Spanish finances when, in November 1568, storm-battered Spanish ships were chased by privateers and sought shelter in the ports of Devon and Cornwall. These ships had 400,000 florins on board as payment for Alva's army. This episode ended with the Queen deciding to take advantage of the money herself. It was, in fact, the property of Genoese financiers. So why should Elizabeth not take over the loan instead of the Spanish king? That Elizabeth prevented the money going to Alva is indisputable, but her precise motives are less clear. Some historians have argued that the seizure was dangerous, pointless and piratical; others, that it made sense to create whatever difficulties she could for Alva. The episode should be seen as a piece of opportunism which was risky but justified. Evidence suggests that Cecil identified the advantage to England and to the Protestant cause in general in seizing the treasure, but that the Queen's decision was made only after she had initially agreed to speed the ships on their way to Alva. She was not, therefore, gleefully and instantaneously seizing the first opportunity she could to stir up trouble for Spain. She did not want major conflict with Philip II, and the episode should not be taken as evidence for any such intention. She no doubt wished to make things as difficult for Alva as possible, but seizures of shipping were not uncommon, and the Queen did not expect major repercussions from her action. She had not, however, anticipated the over-reaction of De Spes, Philip's excitable new ambassador. De Spes urged Alva in the strongest terms to seize English ships and property in the Netherlands – even before Elizabeth's decision to take over the loan had been announced. Alva did so with misgivings, and of course the English retaliated by seizing Spanish property in England.

The excommunication of Elizabeth by Pope Pius V in 1570 is discussed fully in Chapter 4, pages 68–70. For our present purposes, it is enough to note that Philip was not consulted by Pius and doubted both its timing and its political wisdom. Nonetheless, he was increasingly ready to encourage plots against Elizabeth, instructing Alva to prepare to send 10,000 troops to England at the time of the Ridolfi Plot of 1571 (see page 139). In her turn, Elizabeth encouraged English privateers to co-operate with Netherlands privateers – the so-called 'Sea Beggars' – in raiding Spanish shipping. This was also the period in which England and France explored possible marriage alliances and concluded the Treaty of Blois (see page 96). But it must not be assumed that England and Spain were now following a new objective of open hostility, with war as the inevitable outcome. By 1573, representatives of Alva and Elizabeth had concluded a treaty (the Convention of Nymegen) for the resumption of trade between Spain and England. The English government also withdrew support from raids on Spanish shipping in the Indies. The explanation for this new accord is simple enough. Spain had been militarily more than successful in the Netherlands, France was submerged in turmoil following the St Bartholomew's Day Massacre and there was little to be gained by supporting the remaining rebels in the provinces. Once again, Elizabeth adapted her foreign policy to circumstances. And circumstances dictated that apparent neutrality was the best policy to follow. It at least avoided open confrontation with Spain. This is why the Queen was prepared to resist pressure from Walsingham and Leicester who wanted to offer help to the increasingly desperate William of Orange. The only help the Queen would agree to was unofficial, such as not interfering when Orange sought to recruit English Protestant volunteers for his cause.

9 England and Spain, 1575–8

> **KEY ISSUES** How far, by 1578, had England been able to achieve the traditional objective of preserving a semi-independent Netherlands? What is revealed about Elizabeth's customary indecisiveness?

However, by 1575, a subtle change in English foreign policy may be identified. Instead of remaining strictly neutral and detached, Elizabeth began to offer herself as a mediator between Orange and the Spanish. This desire to mediate was, of course, purely selfish. Elizabeth suggested a compromise: that the restoration of the 'liberties' of the provinces should be granted in return for the rebels' acceptance of Habsburg rule. This would both make England feel more secure and pamper to Elizabeth's dislike of rebellion in any form. This change in approach was the response to a change in the political and military situation. Quite simply, it seemed for a time as if a new Spanish offensive would either smash the rebels or force them to seek military assistance from the French. Either of these possibilities was deeply worrying from the English point of view. In fact, the situation changed again in 1576 when the unpaid Spanish army mutinied, sacked the city of Antwerp and brought out the whole of the Netherlands in revolt against Spain. The Estates General of the

Netherlands duly met and called for the removal of Spanish troops and the restoration of the provinces' 'liberties'. The terms of this demand, known as the Pacification of Ghent, were exactly what Elizabeth would have wished. It is a sign of her approval that she should immediately offer the Estates a loan of £100,000 if Spain refused to accept the terms.

Spain, in fact, was in no position to refuse. The new Governor-General of the Netherlands, Don John, accepted the terms when he signed the Perpetual Edict early in 1577, and the Spanish army withdrew from the provinces. But the edict was unlikely to live up to its name. Spanish weakness was temporary, but suspicion among the Estates, divided by religion as well as by faction, was more or less permanent. By mid-1577, Spanish armies were back in the Netherlands – and there was a disturbing new element in the conflict. This was the danger of French intervention under the Duke of Anjou (see page 97). Elizabeth's anxiety is well revealed in her offer, not only of an immediate loan of £100,000, but also of English troops if the French did become involved. An envoy was sent to Philip to try to persuade him to keep to the terms of the Pacification, but, given the divisions within the Estates and their defeat by Spanish forces at the battle of Gembloux in 1578, such persuasion was unlikely to be effective: and so it proved. Even so, Elizabeth did not send an army to the Netherlands. Hesitation, fear of the consequences of a war with Spain, contradictory advice from her councillors – all these took their toll. It was safer to pay for the services of a mercenary – John Casimir of the Palatinate – than to commit England to a conflict of uncertain outcome. In the event, Casimir was worse than useless. His troops were mainly German Protestants who passed their time in attacking and desecrating Dutch Catholic churches. This simply fanned the flames of Calvinist and Catholic distrust among the Estates.

The only realistic conclusion to reach is that, by the end of 1578, Elizabeth's foreign policy was in disarray. The objective had been the traditional one: preventing a major continental power from gaining such complete control of the Netherlands that the country might be used as a base for an invasion of England. But nothing Elizabeth had done had contributed towards a successful resolution of the problem in line with English interests. Instead, she had managed to alienate Spain without earning the trust of the Netherlands. The unhappy prospect of a complete Spanish victory loomed. Spanish power was on the increase. In 1580, Philip II had invaded Portugal: within a year, he was King of Portugal and the commander of another splendid fleet. Meanwhile, the new Governor-General, the Duke of Parma, was proving as adept at exploiting the division among the Estates as he was at defeating them in battle. Holland, one of the richest of the provinces, was holding out, but for how long?

If Philip had the means to launch an invasion of England, it seemed as if he also had the will. In 1579 and 1580, he gave some aid to expeditions to Ireland which went with papal blessing. Since there was little to be gained by further protestations of neutrality or offers to mediate over the Netherlands, Elizabeth felt obliged to support a French intervention at the hands of Anjou (see page 98): the lesser of two evils, perhaps. Walsingham reported that the Queen was even prepared to accept the prospect of the replacement of Spanish authority over the Netherlands by that of France. However, the French rejected offers of sovereignty put forward by the Dutch. At last it seemed as if England was going to have to shoulder the burden and uncertainty of full-scale help for the provinces. Yet Elizabeth hesitated still. There were letters prepared that would have sent expeditionary forces to relieve Antwerp – a city in desperate plight – but such was Elizabeth's indecision that she could not bring herself to sign them. It was Philip's action in seizing English shipping in Spanish ports that finally brought Elizabeth to conclude a treaty with the Dutch. Philip may not have intended the ships to be part of an invasion fleet, but it looked like that to the English. Under the provisions of the Treaty of Nonsuch (1585), Elizabeth would send to the Netherlands 5000 troops and 1000 cavalry under an English commander. She was given control of the Netherlands towns of Brill and Flushing as security for the expenditure, but rejected the offer of sovereignty over the provinces. In her view, of course, sovereignty was God-given: subjects had no right to offer it. In addition to the terms of Nonsuch, a fleet under Drake was sent to raid the Spanish shipping of the Caribbean and to release the English ships held by Philip. But it would be a mistake to assume that Elizabeth was now heartily committed to a war with Spain. Even at this stage, she was in contact with Parma in the hope of some compromise.

10 The Expedition to the Netherlands

> **KEY ISSUE** Why did the expedition to the Netherlands fail?

The chronic indecisiveness of the Queen was such that neither Drake nor Leicester – commander of the force destined for the Netherlands – could be certain that their orders might not be revoked at the last moment. Leicester's task would, in any case, have daunted an experienced military administrator and soldier: Leicester was neither. His correspondence with Burghley and Walsingham reveals a man uncertain of his role, constantly short of money and unable to remove either the divisions within the Dutch ranks or the increasing Dutch suspicion of the Queen's intentions. He was well aware of his own limitations as a military commander, and spent much time trying to persuade the Queen to allow the veteran soldier Sir William Pelham to join him. But Pelham owed the Queen money, and she was reluctant to let him go until he had paid up. Poor Leicester was also faced with the furious anger of the Queen when he accepted the title of Governor-General. There was something almost vindictive in the way in which the Queen's fury waxed and waned. Her behaviour – inspired in part by jealousy and in part by the feeling that the title hampered any possible negotiations with Parma – simply added to Leicester's plight. His letters show as much anxiety over the Queen's attitude towards him as they do over the increasingly disastrous military situation. Leicester found himself trying to cope with numbers of towns which were simply defecting to Parma, attracted by the latter's skilful bribery: his 'golden bullets', as contemporaries termed them. In July 1586, Leicester wrote the following letter to the Privy Council:

> 1 If your lordships will know the cause of so sudden defection of these
>   towns, I must pray you to consider withall . . . I find it is not corruption
>   from the prince [of Parma], for he hath little to give; not desire of the
>   Spanish government, for even the papists abhor it; not mislike of being
> 5 under her majesty, or her officers . . . but, indeed, the cause cannot be
>   imagined to be any other than a deep impression in the wiser sort, that
>   her majesty careth not heartily for them . . . For my own part, what a
>   man without money, countenance, or any other sufficient means, in
>   case so broken and tottering every way, may do, I promise to endeav-
> 10 our to do, to the best of my power . . .

In his letters, Leicester is keen to blame everyone but himself. But his own lack of judgement, as much as the Queen's frequent bursts of meanness, contributed to the breakdown of goodwill between the Dutch and the English. A good example is his appointment of Sir William Stanley to command the newly-captured town of Deventer in 1587. Stanley's background made him a less than ideal choice. He was a Catholic, and had fought for the Duke of Alva as a mercenary. The Estates General protested to no avail, and Stanley repaid Leicester's trust by handing the town over to the Spanish.

A review of the situation in late 1587 reveals unrelieved failure. Leicester had returned for the second and last time to England. The Queen had spent considerable sums of money, but had never showed any awareness of the need to spend more when the occasion demanded it. She had chosen the wrong person to represent her in the Netherlands, and had failed to support him properly when he got there. Elizabeth's on-off negotiations with Parma had yielded no results, and the Spanish were making military preparations for the invasion of England. It may even be that the English involvement in the Netherlands played a substantial part in the Spanish decision to invade England. A successful invasion would, at the very least, leave the Netherlands without allies. In fact, Philip's instructions to his military commanders reveal that he had no intention of annexing England to the Spanish empire. His terms for peace after victory were to be an English withdrawal from the Netherlands and toleration for English Catholics. Thanks in large measure to the Queen's actions, the country faced the prospect of an invasion. Was it not the most fundamental aim of foreign policy to avoid just such an occurrence? Of course, to assess the scale of the Queen's miscalculations requires an appreciation of the likelihood of a successful Spanish invasion.

11 1588: The Armada and After

> **KEY ISSUES** Where the aims of the Armada realistic? Why did the proposed invasion fail?

It is ironic that what saved the Netherlands from Parma was, in part at least, a diverting of attention towards the projected invasion of England – together with increasing Spanish involvement in the troubled affairs of France (see pages 98–9). Parma was ordered to hold back on any further Netherlands campaigns in readiness to link up with the Armada – the huge Spanish fleet that was to protect the Duke's crossing from Flanders to Kent. Parma's men were to cross in flat-bottomed boats. There were roughly 17,000 troops in the Flanders invasion force, to be supplemented by about 6000 from the Armada once a footing had been won on English soil.

The Armada did not, of course, succeed. But to what extent was this the fault of the plan itself? Its success depended on the Armada clearing all Dutch and English naval opposition, on excellent communications between Parma and Medina Sidonia, on preparedness on the part of both dukes, on good weather and on precise timing (high tide was needed to embark the troops). The absence of any one of these factors could lead to failure. The invasion of England was, therefore, always a massive gamble, with disaster being more likely than success.

By July 1588, the Armada had entered the Channel. It faced a formidable opponent in the English fleet. Thanks in large part to the reforms of John Hawkins, treasurer to the navy, the fleet was manoeuvrable and well armed. This had been proved by the success of Francis Drake's Cadiz mission in 1587 which had damaged many Spanish ships in harbour and delayed the Armada for a year. In particular, the English had 153 long-range guns as against the Armada's 21. This advantage would not allow the English to blow the Armada out of the water, but it did prevent the Spanish from using their favourite tactic of boarding the opponent's ships. The Armada found it impossible to clear the English from the Channel. Indeed, the English fleet, under Admiral Howard and Francis Drake, was largely undamaged when the Armada anchored off Calais on 27 July.

Under these circumstances, Parma was unwilling to attempt a

crossing. The problem was not simply the continued presence of the English. The Dutch were similarly undefeated at sea, and would relish the chance to attack the Duke's slow-moving barges. Medina Sidonia hoped that Parma would take advantage of what uncertain protection the Armada could offer and risk the crossing. But he was unsure of Parma's exact whereabouts and state of readiness, and Parma was in no hurry to enlighten him. In the midst of this uncertainty, the English sent fire-ships against the anchored Armada. Medina Sidonia, operating on the reasonable assumption that these were the familiar floating bombs, ordered the Armada to set sail immediately. Some ships cut their anchors – an action that proved disastrous when the Armada had to face bad weather in the weeks to come. On 29 July, the battle of Gravelines took place off the coast of Flanders. The Spanish tried to get close enough to the English fleet to board, and the English peppered the Armada from as far away as possible. The English tactics proved most effective. Only three Spanish ships were disabled, but Medina Sidonia had no choice but to pull his fleet out of the fight. The prevailing wind sent the Armada around the north of Scotland and the west of Ireland. Gales, coupled with the loss of so many anchors, sank half the battered fleet. The contemporary English view – 'the Lord blew and they were scattered' – is at least accurate in giving the weather the credit for the destruction of so much of the invasion fleet. Had the Spanish possessed a deep-water port in the Netherlands where they could have sought shelter and the chance to re-fit, then the superiority of English gunnery would have counted for little.

To complete the assessment of the gravity of the threat posed by the Armada, it is also necessary to consider how Parma would have coped with English troops fighting on their own soil had the Armada successfully carried out its task. Against the 23,000 Habsburg forces would have been the south coast militia of roughly 27,000 infantry and 2500 cavalry, together with the army of 16,500 under the command of Leicester at Tilbury. There would also have been a total of 16,000 troops as a bodyguard for Elizabeth herself. This does not take into account other militia in the north. However, this superiority in numbers may be misleading. Elizabeth lacked the resources to put a professional, Habsburg-style army into the field. It is true that there had been attempts in the 1570s to improve the organisation of military training in England, but these steps had affected no more than one tenth of the militia. Money for training and mustering forces mainly came from gentlemen whose patriotism was tempered by the desire to avoid paying tax. Even Burghley himself chose to pay a subsidy assessed as if his income was £133.6s, instead of the many thousands which represented his true worth. The militia was, therefore, underfunded and ill prepared to face an experienced army led by one of the acknowledged masters of the art of warfare. It is as well, therefore, that the English were not put to the test. On the other hand, Parma was by no means confident. In March 1588, he had written to Philip:

1 Even if the Armada supplies us with the 6,000 Spaniards as agreed – and
they are the sinews of the undertaking – I shall still have too few troops
… If I set foot on shore, it will be necessary for us to fight battle after
battle. I shall, of course, lose men by wounds and sickness. I must leave
5 the port and town garrisons strongly defended, to keep open my lines
of communication: and in a very short time my force will thus be so
much reduced as to be quite inadequate to cope with the great multi-
tude of enemies.

12 The Strength of English Sea Power

The failure of the Armada should not lead to an over-estimate of the
naval strength of England. Elizabeth's use of the navy as a weapon of
war was limited by the fact that she could not afford to maintain a professional force. The problem was that most expeditions were, at least
in part, privately financed. This meant that commanders were primarily interested in plunder and tended to disregard orders when
these conflicted with the possibility of obtaining rich pickings elsewhere. For example, in 1589, Drake and Norris were in charge of a
considerable invasion force aimed at provoking a revolt against Philip
II as King of Portugal. Elizabeth had contributed some £49,000 to the
venture, but the rest of the cost was borne by merchants anticipating
profit. Additionally, the commanders were instructed to destroy what
was left of the battered Armada in Santander and San Sebastian and
then to intercept Spanish treasure-ships in the Azores. What actually
happened was that, when the Portuguese in Lisbon failed to rebel, the
planned attack on the Armada was conveniently forgotten: the fact
that the venture was partly funded by merchants was not. The English
fleet set sail for the Azores and the joys of plunder. However,
unfavourable winds prevented the fleet from reaching its destination.
On return to Plymouth, the casualty list was over 11,000. This was a
heavy price to pay for a complete failure. Similarly, when Hawkins
devised a plan to stop the flow of Spanish treasure from her overseas
colonies back to mainland Spain, this so-called 'silver blockade' had
to rely upon the uncoordinated attacks of privateers rather than on
concerted action by an English fleet. This might be occasionally profitable – and some of the money found its way into Elizabeth's treasury
– but it was too haphazard to be fully effective. Although the loss of
over 1000 Spanish and Portuguese vessels in the 1590s can only have
further weakened the over-stretched economy of Spain, what might a
concerted campaign have achieved?

    In addition, these raids did not prevent the building of two
more Armadas in the 1590s. In 1597, the English fleet was so ill
prepared that the Spanish – *en route* to Ireland – had a clear run
through the Channel. Storms came to the rescue of England on
both occasions.

13 Conclusion

> **KEY ISSUES** What changes had taken place in the aims of
> Elizabeth's foreign policy? How successful was that policy, and to
> what may success be attributed?

By the time of Philip II's death in 1598, Spain had been badly mauled in the Netherlands conflict. The Dutch had exploited the mutinous condition of unpaid Spanish troops and had brought off impressive victories which safeguarded the northern provinces (now known as the United Provinces) against the increasingly bankrupt Spanish. As for the French, Henry IV had concluded the triple alliance with the United Provinces and England in 1596 (see page 99). By 1598, France and Spain were at peace but in a state of mutual hatred that was music to English ears. The conflict between England and Spain continued until 1604, when James I, Elizabeth's successor, brought it to an end.

On one level, Elizabeth would seem to have achieved most of her foreign policy aims and objectives. She had avoided an invasion by a foreign power, be it Habsburg Spain or France of the Guises. England had not been yoked to another country in such a way as to lose her independence of action. Unlike Spain, the Crown did not, despite its debts, go bankrupt. But economic depression caused by the cessation of Anglo-Spanish trade combined with war taxation to create real resentment in England: resentment which is revealed in the increasingly quarrelsome and disenchanted attitude of Parliament in the final years of the reign. On the other hand, it is true that the war with Spain offered men of capital the opportunity of great reward through privateering. Profits and expertise acquired through raids on Spanish colonies and shipping laid the foundations for such enterprises as the East India Company (1600) and others founded in the reign of James I, such as the Virginia Company (1606) and the Newfoundland Company (1610). In this sense, it is possible to argue that Elizabeth's policies did meet the aim of maintaining English economic interests – at least in the long term, and for the few.

There were major changes in the Queen's objectives as the reign progressed. The assumption that France was the natural enemy was found wanting when Spain offered the greatest threat to the Netherlands. Increasing enmity with Spain and increasing co-operation with the French reflected this change. But the constant objective was to ensure that the Netherlands had sufficient independence for English commerce and security to be maintained. This objective was largely achieved. Although the southern Netherlands remained under Spanish control, the northern provinces did not. It is, however, difficult to assess how far the Queen's actions contributed to this satisfactory result. Philip II felt that English involvement was sufficiently disruptive to justify the expense and danger of the Armada. The

Dutch themselves were less convinced of the value of Elizabeth's hesitant and unenthusiastic assistance. In military terms, English help was of dubious value – and for this the Queen was in large part responsible. Leicester was the wrong choice as military commander, and the Queen's treatment of him was unlikely to overcome his defects. Nor were her rather desperate attempts to negotiate with Parma on the eve of all-out war with Spain likely to endear her to the Dutch. These attempts demonstrate not only that Elizabeth had no enthusiasm for full-scale conflict with Spain, but also that she would have avoided it if possible. They also demonstrate her awareness of the real danger of such conflict.

It has to be said that England was fortunate to escape the worst conceivable consequences of her war with Spain: namely, Spanish troops on English soil. It is difficult to avoid the conclusion that the successes of Elizabethan foreign policy owed much to luck and circumstances beyond the Queen's control. Convenient assassination, mistaken decisions by adversaries, helpful weather and Spanish bankruptcy were Elizabeth's allies. They were the kind of allies she liked: they made no financial demands.

Some historians have argued that Elizabeth had aims above and beyond those occasioned purely by narrow self-interest: aims which represented a break with the traditional policies of predecessors. Simon Adams' view[3] is that Elizabeth was motivated by the desire to see Protestant subjects granted freedom of conscience by their Catholic rulers. This, he has suggested, is the explanation behind her complicated relationship with the Dutch and her curiously hesitant manner of assisting them. There is some truth in this, but it is unlikely that Elizabeth wished to secure such freedom solely or primarily as a matter of principle. Her religious policy in England avoided persecution only when it was to her political advantage, and political advantage, rather than an attachment to the principle of toleration, lies behind her wish to see Philip II grant religious liberty to the Calvinists of the Netherlands. Such toleration would be an obstacle to that complete Spanish control of the provinces which Elizabeth's foreign policy constantly strove to prevent.

Elizabeth had, of course, little sympathy for the views of those councillors who tried to add a new aim to English foreign policy: the defence and furtherance of international Protestantism. The Queen's lack of enthusiasm was probably fortunate, since the country lacked the resources to maintain the position of Protestant champion on the scale envisaged by the zealots. That lack of enthusiasm may have reflected her dislike of aiding and abetting rebels, but it did not prevent her from supporting them. After all, she did provide military assistance in the Netherlands, Scotland and France for those fighting against legitimate monarchs. That she did so is a testimony to the extent to which English foreign policy was not only obliged to respond to events beyond its control, but also to follow short-term objectives which were frequently dangerous and as frequently distasteful to Elizabeth herself.

Finally, it is possible to identify tentatively one crucial development in foreign policy which separated Elizabeth's reign from the past: Elizabethan foreign policy did not operate to serve the monarch's personal or dynastic glory. This is not to say that Elizabeth did not regard her own interests as paramount: it was simply that she had no place on the battlefield. War suited the extravagant posturings of Henry VIII. It did not suit the Virgin Queen.

References

1   G.D. Ramsay, 'The Foreign Policy of Elizabeth I' in C. Haigh, *The Reign of Elizabeth I* (London, 1984). Ramsay provides a very useful insight into the mechanics of sixteenth-century diplomacy.
2   For a revealing discussion of the matrimonial negotiations, see S. Doran, *Monarchy & Matrimony: the courtships of Elizabeth I* (London, 1996).
3   There are two articles by Simon Adams that are well worth consulting: 'Faction, Clientage and Party: English Politics, 1550–1603' in *History Today* 32 (1982), pp.33–9 and 'The Lurch into War', *History Today* (May 1988).

Summary Diagram
Elizabeth, France and Spain

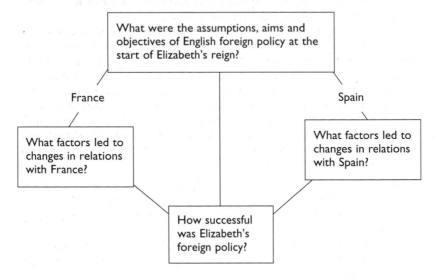

Working on Chapter 5

This is a lengthy and detailed chapter. Notes should be focused on the following themes:
What changes can be identified in English foreign policy aims over the period, and what factors governed those changes?
Given the varying aims, how successfully were they achieved?

The best way to tackle this would be to plot a time-line through the period using columns for the date/event, the aims (including the reasons for them) and the extent of success. This will allow you to explore change and also to identify how far changes in policy followed from events.

Answering structured and essay questions on Chapter 5

Essay questions generally fall into two types. One type is the wide-ranging question on general foreign policy; in this case, although France and Spain will dominate the essay, you should also refer to Ireland and Scotland (see Chapter 6). The second type usually deals specifically with France or Spain or the Netherlands.

The first type will, in all probability, ask for a critical assessment of Elizabeth's performance. A good understanding of Elizabeth's aims and objectives is central to an effective essay.

There are a number of the 'challenging statement'-type questions in the list below. Students often feel that 'getting into' essays of this type is the hardest part, and this is why many of the guidance sections in this book have concentrated on what is needed for an effective introduction. You will recall that advice was given on standard phrases to help overcome the difficulty, such as 'I intend to argue that ...'. Don't forget that your argument must recognise both its own limitations and also possible alternative views. It has been suggested that the phrase 'On the other hand ...' can prove useful. Try out this technique on questions 1 and 3 below.

1. 'Elizabeth's successes in foreign affairs owed more to luck than to any other single factor.' How far do you agree with this statement?
2. What were Elizabeth's aims in foreign policy? How successfully were they achieved?
3. 'Elizabeth's foreign policy was inconsistent because she had no clear aims and so simply reacted to crises as and when they occurred.' How far do you agree with this statement?
4. How and why did Elizabethan foreign policy change in the course of the Queen's reign?
5. What factors influenced the conduct of Elizabethan foreign policy?

Question 5 is reasonably straightforward, but may lead the unwary into some confusion. Most students are aware that historians generally find it helpful to consider 'factors' under headings like 'economic', 'religious', 'political' and so on. However, it would be tricky to attempt to handle question 5 in this manner. Such factors are better suited to topics dealing with *causes*. After all, although the traditional objective in the Netherlands was partly economic, it was also partly political and, given the Reformation, partly religious as well. So the best method is to adapt the 'aims and objectives' approach. But you will also need to discuss, not only who controlled foreign policy, but also the extent to which specific policies were frequently a response to factors outside English control. It is often a good idea to give an indication of which aspects were most important. For example, it is clear that the Netherlands tended to dominate English thinking and efforts.

The second type of question will similarly demand an assessment of Elizabeth's policies, although with greater and more specific detail. It would be very unwise to revise for the general foreign policy essay only and leave yourself ill equipped for the narrower essay. Below is a list of the likely topics. It is suggested that you make up a list of essay titles yourself. Aim to do at least three per topic. Remember that any essay question must give the candidate the opportunity to argue a case.

1. The Netherlands
2. France
3. Spain
4. The Armada

Finally, remember that good candidates often attack the assumptions of the question. After all, the introduction to this chapter suggested that 'foreign policy' was, to an extent, an inappropriate term to use given the lack of real knowledge of other countries and the amateurish diplomacy as practised by the courts of Europe.

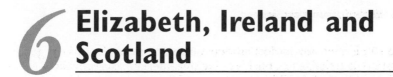

6 Elizabeth, Ireland and Scotland

POINTS TO CONSIDER

The good news is that this chapter is markedly less complex in terms of detail than its predecessor. When reading it for the first time you can adopt a similar approach to the one you adopted when reading Chapter 5. Look out for answers to the following four questions:
What were the criteria for a successful English policy?
How successful was that policy?
How far was religion an issue in Elizabeth's policies towards Ireland and Scotland?
What links can be made between events and policies concerning France and Spain and those concerning Ireland and Scotland?

KEY DATES

1541	Henry VIII declared King of Ireland by Act of Parliament.
1548	France dispatched 10,000 troops to Scotland. Mary Stuart taken to France.
1558	Knox published *The First Blast of the Trumpet*.
1559	Rebellion of the Lords of the Congregation.
1560	English army sent to Scotland. Treaty of Edinburgh: French troops withdrew from Scotland.
1561	Mary Stuart returned to Scotland from France.
	Sussex campaigned against Shane O'Neill in Ireland.
1565	Mary Stuart married Darnley.
1566	Murder of Riccio.
	Birth of James, son of Mary Stuart.
1567	Murder of Darnley. Mary Stuart married Bothwell. Forced to renounce throne in favour of infant James.
	Shane O'Neill killed.
1568	Mary Stuart fled to England.
1569	Norfolk marriage plot.
	Revolt of the northern earls.
	Fitzmaurice/Edmund Butler uprising in Ireland.
1571	Ridolfi plot discovered.
	Smith's ill-fated Ulster plantation launched.
1579	Fitzmaurice and Sander landed in Smerwick, triggering uprisings in Ireland.
1583	Throckmorton Plot.
1585	Parry Plot.
1586	Babington Plot discovered.
1587	Execution of Mary Stuart.
1593	Hugh O'Neill, Earl of Tyrone, elected to title of 'The O'Neill'.

1596-7 Spanish armadas to Ireland scattered by storms.
1598 Battle of Yellow Ford: Hugh O'Neill defeated English forces.
Munster plantation destroyed.
1599 Essex appointed Lord Lieutenant in Ireland. Left Ireland later in
year.
1600 Mountjoy Lord Deputy in Ireland.
1601 Spanish army landed at Kinsale. Mountjoy defeated Hugh O'Neill.
1603 Days after the death of Elizabeth I, O'Neill submitted to
Mountjoy.

1 Ireland in the Sixteenth Century: Land and People

KEY ISSUE How similar were the Irish and English social and political systems?

1 The custom of these savages is to live as the brute beasts among the
mountains ... They carry on a perpetual war with the English, who here
keep garrison for the Queen ... The chief inclination of these people is
to be robbers, and to plunder each other; so that no day passes with-
5 out a call to arms among them ... These people call themselves
Christians. Mass is said among them, and regulated according to the
orders of the Church of Rome. The great majority of their churches,
monasteries, and hermitages, have been demolished by the hands of the
English ... In short, in this kingdom there is neither justice nor right, and
10 everyone does what he pleases.

So said Captain Cuellar, a survivor from the Spanish Armada ship-
wrecked in 1588 on the coasts of Ireland. He clearly felt that the Irish
he encountered were beyond the pale of civilisation. Of course, the
frightened, uncomprehending and mistreated Cuellar was in no position to make an objective assessment of the Irish as he sought desperately through the marshes and forests of the most remote and
poorest parts of Ireland for refuge and a passage back to Spain. But
Englishmen new to Ireland frequently shared Cuellar's opinion. As
they looked out on Gaelic Ireland – the Ireland relatively free of
English influence – they also felt confused and threatened by a society
they did not understand. And, like Cuellar, they concluded that the
Gaelic Irish were uncivilised. The vantage point of these Englishmen
was the Irish territory belonging to the kings of England: the area
around Dublin known as the Pale. Indeed, the phrase 'beyond the
pale' – as used earlier in this paragraph – carries with it the meaning
of an area outside the bounds of civilisation.

So Ireland was disturbingly different from England. The Pale itself
had many of the hallmarks of English society – superficially. The
monarch's authority was represented in the Pale by a Lord Lieutenant

Ireland in the sixteenth century

or Lord Deputy. There were law courts in Dublin practising English law, and an Irish parliament summoned in the manner of its English counterpart (though even less frequently). The gentry of the Pale prided themselves on their 'Englishness' and sent sons to be educated at the Inns of Court in London. But the Gaelic language was no stranger to the Pale or to the 'Old English' gentry, and the yeoman class – so characteristic of the English county – was entirely absent. Outside the Pale were the 'Old English' feudal lords. Descendants of the Norman conquerors of Ireland, they were virtually kings in their own lands. Their allegiance to the English Crown was tempered by this near autocratic power. If it suited them to respond to calls for military assistance from Dublin, then they did so. If it did not, then they used their private armies of retainers and mercenaries to pursue private feuds. These nobles therefore occupied a middle-ground between the Pale and Gaelic Ireland. Some of them were more *hibernicised* – close to Gaelic society – than others. Rivalries between great Anglo-Irish earls would often be fed by the closeness of their links with one or other of the cultures. One Earl of Desmond, for example, had been found guilty of treason in 1467: his condemnation and execution came about in part because of his over-identification with Gaelic chieftains. The bitter enemies of the Fitzgeralds of Desmond were the Butlers, the head of whose family was the Earl of Ormond and who were, in turn, pro-English.

The map on page 117 shows just how much of Ireland was under the control of Gaelic chieftains. These chieftains generally refused to accept the authority of the kings of England. Gaelic, and not English, law was in force in their territories. Of the many differences between the two legal systems, the most significant related to the inheritance of land and title. The English system was that of primogeniture. On the death of an English earl, for example, the eldest son – or daughter, if there were no male children – inherited all landed property. In the Gaelic system, the chieftain did not own the land he controlled: he was not a landlord in the English sense. The territory – apart from some allotted to the chieftain by virtue of his title – belonged to the freemen as a whole. It was periodically redistributed amongst them. Nor did the chieftain pass his title down to his eldest son by right. A successor – known as the 'Tanist' – was elected by the freemen, who could chose whom they wished from the members of the ruling family. The election would generally take place before the death of the chieftain to ensure an orderly succession. In fact the system frequently stimulated, rather than curbed, violence.

Gaelic Ireland was remarkably localised even by the standards of contemporary England. Communications between lordships were often non-existent. Chieftains travelled with an armed retinue as much for protection as for display even within their own territories. Towns were few and far between: the economy depended largely on barter, and wealth was measured in livestock. The movement of cattle to and from pasture land in winter and summer was inevitably accompanied by the movement of people. This gave English newcomers the feeling that the Gaelic Irish were nomads, and unspeakably primitive and inferior to boot. Small wonder, then, that where English customs and Gaelic customs met, confusion (at the very least) would ensue. Mutual incomprehension does not easily engender peaceable relations.

2 Ireland and the Monarchs of England

KEY ISSUE What changes were made by Henry VIII to the English kings' traditional policy of relying on a deputy in Ireland?

Until the reign of Henry VIII, English kings generally relied upon a deputy – one of the great Anglo-Irish earls – to maintain the interests of the Crown in Ireland. The advantage of this system was that a man such as the Earl of Kildare had power and influence which transcended the divisions between English society and Gaelic society. But, by the 1530s, this reliance on a great feudal lord had been brought into question in two respects. Firstly, the Anglo-Irish earls were all too reminiscent of the over-mighty subjects whose power had been demonstrated with disastrous consequences in the Wars of the Roses. Henry VII had succeeded in making service to the Crown and influence at court, rather than ownership of land, the benchmarks of status. To invest an Anglo-Irish earl with near-absolute authority was outmoded. Secondly, the Henrician Reformation made it particularly dangerous. After all, the break with Rome brought Ireland to the European stage. Foreign enemies of Henry VIII and his Protestant successors could use Ireland, its loyalty to Roman Catholicism and its Gaelic dissent as a potent weapon against England: either as a springboard for invasion of England or as a means of tying down English troops and thereby sabotaging the economy of the country. To rely upon a deputy who was an Anglo-Irish Catholic lord with Gaelic connections might seem, at best, imprudent.

Henry VIII responded to the potential threat in two ways. Firstly, direct rule from London replaced delegation to over-mighty Anglo-Irish subjects. Lord Lieutenants or Deputies were chosen, not from the Anglo-Irish earls or the Old English of the Pale, but from London courtiers. Secondly, the King chose to change his title from 'Lord of Ireland' to 'King of Ireland'. The adoption of the title of king paved the way towards an attempt to anglicise Gaelic chieftains. By the system known as 'surrender and regrant', a chieftain handed over the territory he controlled to the King. He then received it back with the title of English earl and the chance to pass on the land and title by primogeniture. This was unlikely to 'civilise' Ireland in the short term and would, of course, cause resentment among the freemen. What right, they might justly ask, had the chieftain to surrender land belonging to the clan as a whole? And, if the new earl subsequently fell foul of the King, what right had the King to confiscate that land?

3 Elizabeth and Ireland: Problems and Possible Solutions

> **KEY ISSUES** What difficulties did Ireland pose from Elizabeth's perspective at the start of her reign? How might those difficulties be tackled?

Historians – and examiners – frequently ask the question 'How successfully did Elizabeth handle the problems posed by Ireland to England itself?' The first stage in making such an assessment is to summarise the problems facing the Queen at the start of her reign. Once this has been done, it will be possible to evaluate her responses.

Firstly, given the clash of English and Gaelic cultures, Ireland lacked any central authority. Secondly, the traditional system of allowing over-mighty subjects to govern in the monarch's name had been found wanting. Thirdly, the post-Reformation English monarchy had to beware lest Ireland became a pawn in a Europe-wide conflict. For Elizabeth, there were certain uncomfortable parallels with Spain and the Netherlands (see page 101). Fourthly, the attempts made by Henry VIII to extend the Crown's influence over Gaelic Ireland had been largely unsuccessful. Fifthly, Ireland was expensive, since it was becoming increasingly obvious that a standing army under the control of London would be necessary to maintain English interests. Sixthly, the imposition of a deputy from England was likely to cause resentment among the 'Old English' of the Pale and beyond.

It would be tempting to assume that no flesh-and-blood monarch of England could possibly 'solve' the problems posed by Ireland. But England had certain enormous advantages when dealing with her sister island. Most importantly, she had a much larger population and vastly greater resources. This meant that an English monarch could, in the last resort, raise an army in England which no Gaelic chieftain or Anglo-Irish lord could hope to meet in formal battle with any chance of success. Even if a guerrilla campaign were to be fought against such an army, little could be done to prevent the English from destroying the crops and livestock which meant both life and wealth to Gaelic society.

How much of a threat to the English monarch's rule in Ireland was Irish nationalism? Given a Protestant king or queen of England, such nationalism might well be fuelled by the loyal Catholicism of Ireland.

But, of course, the intense localism and traditional independence of Gaelic society offset the potentially unifying factor of religion. It would be misleading – even anachronistic – to speak of Gaelic nationalism at the start of Elizabeth's reign.

It could be argued that Elizabeth had three possible courses of action in handling challenges posed by Ireland. Firstly, she might ignore the rest of Ireland – that is, most of Gaelic Ireland – beyond the Pale and the southern counties. But both the internal and the international situation made this extremely inadvisable. The endemic violence and ambitions of chieftains in Ireland meant that the areas under English influence would be constantly under threat. More importantly, as we have seen, the religious and political crises of Europe meant that Ireland could never be a mere matter of domestic policy for England. Secondly, Elizabeth could attempt to colonise areas where English influence was limited or non-existent. This might prove attractive to Old English or the land-hungry English of the mainland. This would also pander to English views of the Gaelic Irish as barbarians and justify colonisation as a gift of civilisation. But the Gaels were, of course, unlikely to see colonies in this light. Colonies would, therefore, need to be defended by a system of fortresses or garrison towns to be secure against Gaelic attack. The third option was a full-scale military conquest. This would not be easy given the Gaelic preference for guerrilla warfare, and would need to be followed up with a system of fortresses and/or colonisation. The second and third options, in order to be successful, would require long-term planning and very substantial investment.

The following sections seek to examine the policies pursued by Elizabeth, giving due regard to the nature of the problems and potential solutions.

4 Shane O'Neill

> **KEY ISSUES** In what ways did Shane O'Neill pose a threat to Elizabeth's authority in Ireland? How effective was Elizabeth's treatment of O'Neill? What was Elizabeth's response to O'Neill's downfall?

The career of Shane O'Neill provides the historian with an excellent opportunity to study the way in which Elizabeth tackled the problems posed by Ireland. Under the 'surrender and re-grant' policy, Shane's father, Con O'Neill, had abandoned his Gaelic title of 'The O'Neill', had promised to adopt the English language and habits, had surrendered 'his' lands and had been granted them back with the title of Earl of Tyrone. The O'Neill base was in Ulster – an area remote from English influence. But Shane had been chosen as his father's tanist in defiance of the English law of primogeniture, which made the eldest son, Matthew, heir to his father's title and earldom. In the event, Shane instigated the murder of Matthew and Con was forced out of Tyrone. By 1561, Shane had been proclaimed a rebel by the Earl of Sussex, the Lord Deputy, but the former's military strength – increased by his use of Scottish mercenaries and his unprecedented step of arming peasants – meant that Sussex could do little until reinforcements arrived from England. However, once they arrived, Shane could not risk a formal battle. His guerrilla tactics of ambush and retreat were irritating to Sussex, but they could not prevent the Lord Deputy from marching through Shane's territories and slaughtering enormous numbers of livestock. This exhibition of power caused Shane to negotiate an audience with the Queen, who was treated to a display of Gaelic court manners which astounded the English courtiers and emphasised very clearly the gulf between the two cultures. But O'Neill's howling and pleading in the traditional manner was not the sign of a defeated man. What, then, could Elizabeth do with him? To defeat him militarily would involve massive expenditure: and, even then, success could not be guaranteed. In any case, it has been made abundantly clear in previous chapters that massive expenditure and Elizabeth were uneasy bedfellows. She therefore tried the risky stratagem of curbing Shane by giving him an important role as a servant of the English Crown. He was encouraged to oust Scottish settlements in Ulster – always a thorn in the side of the English, given the strained relations between Scotland and England. But it is hard to see how using Shane in this way was likely to tame him. There was little that Elizabeth could realistically offer him that he would value. Sussex recognised this, and tried to solve the problem by bringing Shane to battle after the latter's return to Ireland. Indecisive skirmishing duly followed, and the Lord Deputy had little alternative but to make a treaty with O'Neill. Extraordinarily enough, the treaty accepted him as 'The O'Neill' in the Gaelic fashion. That this was a humiliation for the government is evident from a failed attempt to murder Shane with a poisoned cask of wine. No-one was under any illusions as to the danger posed by Shane. He had attempted to negotiate for French military assistance by offering the crown of Ireland to Charles IX, had also negotiated with Mary Queen of Scots and, for good measure, had sought to pose as a defender of the faith against Protestant heresy.

It could, however, be argued that the greater armed strength of England proved indirectly to be Shane's downfall. In 1566, Sussex's successor, Sir Henry Sidney, pursued the standard tactic of marching through O'Neill's land causing as much devastation and capturing as many fortresses as possible. To recoup some of his losses, Shane attacked the O'Donnells of Tyrconnell, but his forces were badly mauled at the battle of Farsetmore (1567). It is a mark of his desperation that he appealed for help to the MacDonnells – bitter enemies some two years before. A meeting with them degenerated into a squalid brawl and Shane's miserable death. His head – thoughtfully pickled for the journey – was sent to Dublin.

No doubt Elizabeth's government was more than pleased to hear of Shane's fate, with or without his pickled remains. But they had less reason to feel self-satisfied as it was ill luck, poor judgement and his own excesses that had brought Shane to his sordid end. Nevertheless, the downfall of Shane O'Neill had two major consequences for Elizabeth's Irish policy. Firstly, it gave her the chance to reassert royal claims to Ulster as a whole. In 1569, an Act of Attainder (legalising the confiscation of the lands of rebels) abolished the title of 'The O'Neill'. Secondly, Shane's death gave the government the chance to plant colonies in Ulster – the first attempt so to do in Elizabeth's reign.

5 Control by Colonisation: The Failure of the Ulster Plantation, 1572–6

> **KEY ISSUES** What was the main aim of colonisation? Why did the Ulster plantation fail?

Colonisation should be seen as a mechanism for conquering Gaelic Ireland. However, the attempts to colonise Ulster in the 1570s were expensive failures and demonstrate the lack of a precise blueprint or detailed planning in the government's strategy. In Elizabeth's eyes, one advantage of the proposed colonisation was that it was to be undertaken by private individuals, albeit with some financial support from the Crown. But it is clear that these attempts were simply not thought through. Elizabeth gave official sanction to a plan by Sir Thomas Smith – a member of her Privy Council – to establish a colony in the Ards peninsula. She granted Smith lands which belonged to the O'Neills of Clandeboy. To ignore the rights of Sir Brian McPhelim O'Neill was foolhardy, and the colonists, under the direction of Smith's illegitimate son, lacked the military muscle to survive in the face of attacks from Sir Brian. After the murder of his son in 1573, Smith had to hand the enterprise over to Walter Devereux, Earl of Essex. Essex had greater resources – some of which came from the Queen – but relied like Smith on the efforts of land-hungry English adventurers who needed rapid success to maintain their enthusiasm. The Queen likewise demanded swift results without providing Essex with the support he needed for an overwhelming military victory. Elizabeth even demanded that Essex abandon the enterprise if he failed to make it pay its own way: a curious attitude to what was, after all, a major military campaign. Essex left a trail of massacres and damage behind him, but, in an area where there were few towns and against an enemy who refused to fight set-piece battles, Essex came to the sensible conclusion that only fortress garrisons could subdue Ulster. In this, the Queen agreed, but failed to provide the funds needed fully to implement the scheme.

By 1576, Essex had exhausted himself to little effect. The Queen granted him the title of Earl Marshal of Ireland, but it was no consolation for his crippling losses and failures. Sickness and depression brought him to his death-bed in Dublin. His failure marked the abandonment of colonisation by private enterprise. Indeed, the whole episode simply increased the bitterness and suspicion with which the English and Gaels regarded each other. For this, Elizabeth must accept much of the blame.

6 Control by Colonisation: The Plantation of Munster, from 1568

> **KEY ISSUES** Why did rebellions break out under Butler and Fitzmaurice? Why was the Munster plantation ultimately unsuccessful?

Munster was a more attractive proposition for English adventurers than Ulster. It was richer, more fertile and considerably more accessible. Indeed, it had received earlier attention from land-hungry English than had Ulster. Men such as Sir Peter Carew (pronounced Carey) from Devon were not concerned with the rights of Gaels or Old English if they could get their hands on land. In 1568, Carew launched a series of aggressive claims against certain gentry in the Pale itself, as well as in Munster, based on the alleged holdings of one of his Norman ancestors. Carew had the support of the English Lord Deputy and the Privy Council. The encouragement of this naked aggression could only increase tension between the English government, the 'New English' colonists and the Old English.

In 1569, rebellion broke out as a direct result of the resentment caused by English policy. The motives of Sir Edmund Butler, a member of the generally pro-English House of Ormond, were clearly to destroy the small English plantations – Carew's in particular. What is significant is that Butler collaborated with Gaelic chieftains: a testimony to the depth of his resentment, caused largely by the remarkable insensitivity of Elizabethan policy. The rebellion was stamped out, as was a revolt under James Fitzmaurice Fitzgerald (referred to below as Fitzmaurice), but the latter sought not only to establish common cause with Gaelic Ireland, but also to convert rebellion into a crusade against the heretical Queen of England. The combination of anti-English feeling and Catholicism was a potent brew, strengthened as it was by the papal excommunication of Elizabeth in 1570.

However, it is easy to over-estimate the support aroused by the call of religion. Perhaps it was a useful justification for rebellion, but, if so, was probably a less important factor than the hatred of English adventurers.

By the end of the decade, Fitzmaurice had returned with a small, papal-sponsored force. His landing at Smerwick in July 1579 triggered uprisings in Ulster, Leinster and throughout Munster, and brought the dithering Earl of Desmond into rebellion. The new Lord Deputy, Lord Grey, reacted with relentless repression and some savagery. He read a Catholic conspiracy into every act of defiance and resentment: Anglo-Irish and Gael alike were sent to the gallows, whatever their actual motives for opposing the government. His ruthlessness in destroying livestock and harvest brought famine and death throughout Munster. Even the Pale suffered.

The eventual defeat of the rebellions paved the way for a more thorough and systematic colonisation between 1579 and 1583, based in large part upon the confiscated lands of the Desmonds. It is important to note that the loyal Old English were offered few or no opportunities to take advantage of the available land. Instead, lands were touted for sale in England, where the land-hungry younger sons of the Carew type were encouraged to slake their ambitions for the status of great landowners in the rich lands of Munster. Many did so, but the plantations in Munster were largely destroyed in uprisings in 1598. Once again, the government sought to keep its own expenses down by pandering to greed. Adventurers had been encouraged to over-reach themselves. Many had acquired so much land that they were unable to exploit it. Neither Elizabeth nor her advisers had learned much from the mistakes of the Ulster plantations.

7 The Rebellion of Hugh O'Neill, Earl of Tyrone

> **KEY ISSUES** To what extent can Elizabeth's policies be seen as the main reason for Tyrone's rebellion? To what extent was Tyrone effectively defeated?

After the death of Shane O'Neill (see page 123), the government had adopted a cautious approach in Ulster. The old 'surrender and regrant' policy resurfaced, and attempts were made to play one chieftain off against the other to prevent the rise of another dominant lord on the model of Shane. Hugh O'Neill – a grandson of Con O'Neill – was educated as a royal ward and attached to the household of the Earl of Leicester. He was, in time, granted the title of Earl of Tyrone. But Hugh was in a position fraught with difficulty. He was an obvious candidate for the Gaelic title of 'The O'Neill' – an attractive prospect to him. He also liked being an Anglo-Irish noble. However, as time went on, it became clear to him that he lacked influence where it most mattered in Elizabethan England – at court and on the Privy Council. His friends Leicester and Walsingham were dead, and he had no-one who could speak for him at the centre of power. He saw Ireland increasingly at the mercy of relatively minor English officials and adventurers: the title of Earl of Tyrone would not alone enable him to fulfil his ambition of ruling Ulster without interference. His attempt to gain a commission from the Queen to govern Ulster was unsuccessful, and he responded by turning to Gaelic Ireland, where traditional antagonism to English encroachments proved to be a useful weapon. In 1593, he was elected to the title of 'The O'Neill', but followed a less traditional path by building up a far more power-ful and extensively trained fighting force than his predecessors had possessed. By 1595, Tyrone was in open rebellion and looking for help from Spain. Philip II was not one to throw away money on lost causes, but Tyrone's effective and modernised army interested him – especially when it became clear that Elizabeth's forces were finding it a formidable opponent. In 1597, an Armada was dispatched for Ireland, only to be scattered by the winds. Undaunted, Tyrone inflicted a remarkable defeat on a 4000-strong English army at Yellow Ford in 1598. Indeed, it could be argued that the successes of Tyrone revealed the folly of Elizabeth's past meanness. All her parsimonious (penny-pinching), free-enterprise schemes, all the inadequate but still substantial monies provided for the campaigns of Lord Deputies, all the attempts to 'civilise' the Gaelic Irish, all in jeopardy and all potentially wasted. It was at this point that the Munster plantation was virtually swept away. Tyrone was, in effect, at the head of a confeder-ation of Gaels and some Old English who had in common their antag-onism to Elizabeth's policies. Indeed, if Tyrone were to succeed in linking up with a Spanish invasion force. then the English might well be forced back into the Pale and the surrounding southern counties.

The defeat at Yellow Ford so infuriated the Queen that she finally decided to devote sufficient resources to a full-scale military conquest of Ireland. But it was nearly too late. In 1599, the Queen's favourite, Robert Devereux, Earl of Essex, was sent to Ireland with an army of 16,000 infantry and 1300 cavalry. Essex was not a good choice. He achieved nothing. Ireland was not a happy hunting-ground for those who relied upon the affection of the Queen for their position. Essex made a truce with Tyrone and scampered back to London.

The perilous position for the English in Ireland was redeemed only by the appointment of the dour Charles Blount, Lord Mountjoy, as military commander. Landing in 1600, he managed to motivate the dispirited English forces and succeeded in pushing Tyrone back towards Ulster, only to be faced with a formidable Spanish invasion of 3400 crack troops at Kinsale. Turning to besiege Kinsale, Mountjoy ran the risk of finding himself surrounded by Tyrone. It was, indeed, a close-run thing. Tyrone made an error in risking a full-scale battle outside Kinsale, and was heavily defeated by Mountjoy. By January 1602, the Kinsale garrison had surrendered, Munster was well on the way to being pacified and Tyrone was back in Ulster. Hugh O'Neill finally submitted six days after Elizabeth died, but only on generous terms. He was recognised as the Chief Lord of Ulster under the Crown: the very position he had sought and fought to achieve. Elizabeth's successor, James I, was therefore obliged to pursue the old-fashioned and discredited policy of allowing over-mighty subjects to rule Ulster ostensibly in his name.

8 The Irish Reformation

> **KEY ISSUE** Why did Protestantism make so little headway in Ireland?

In 1560, an Act of Uniformity declared Elizabeth to be Supreme Governor of the Church of Ireland – very much on the model of the English Act of 1559 (see page 20). It showed some awareness of the need to bear in mind Irish conditions by permitting priests ignorant of English the use of a Latin version of the prescribed prayer book. However, any assessment of the impact of the Elizabethan religious settlement on Ireland must recognise its essential failure. Conditions were not promising at the very start of the reign. Under Henry VIII, monasteries had been dissolved in the Pale, Ormond lands and the towns of Munster: elsewhere, they continued in existence throughout Elizabeth's reign. The Elizabethan brand of Protestantism was seen by the Irish as nothing more than the religious version of English political encroachments and was treated accordingly. Effective Protestant preachers could not be attracted to Ireland: livings were poor, and the language barrier virtually insurmountable. There was no pool of Protestant clergy available to take the place of religious conservatives. The only meaningful attempt to improve clerical education came with the founding of Trinity College, Dublin as late as 1592.

Even in the Pale, the Old English got round the demands of uniformity by employing Catholic priests as domestic chaplains. Moreover, the enthusiasm of the educated for Counter-Reformation Catholicism was fanned by an increasing supply of seminary priests: partly from Spain and partly from those younger sons of the gentry of the Pale educated at continental universities.

9 Conclusion

KEY ISSUE How successful was Elizabeth's Irish policy?

A reminder of the basic criteria marking a successful Irish policy is now in order. Briefly, there are four major elements. The first is that the government should prevent Ireland from being used by a foreign power as a base for an invasion of England. In this, Elizabeth was successful, although of course she was unable to prevent Spain from landing small invasion forces in Ireland itself. Secondly, Ireland should be controlled in a manner which suited English interests. Ideally, Gaelic Ireland should be increasingly anglicised. In this, Elizabeth's policy was largely a failure. Mountjoy's campaigns may have subdued the country, but it was not pacified in the long term. The net result of this and other policies in the 45 years of Elizabethan rule was that antagonism between England and the Gaelic population was intensified. Even worse, the influx of 'New English' administrators and colonists, operating with government complicity in defiance of the interests of the Old English, effectively alienated many of the traditional loyalists from the country of their origin. Elizabeth had sown the seeds of an Irish nationalism which transcended Gaelic and Anglo-Irish divisions. This meant that any 'solution' in Ireland was likely to be based on military conquest and occupation. Private enterprise colonisation was cheap, but no real alternative. And the longer the Queen delayed in committing adequate funds to military campaigns, the more dangerous the climate became. Tyrone's successes had put in jeopardy almost all English authority outside the Pale and surrounding counties. Mountjoy's victory was impressive precisely because defeat was all too possible.

The imposition of the Elizabethan Protestant religious settlement on Ireland is the third element in any successful policy. After all, religion was a vital weapon in the political control of the country. But here, Elizabeth's failure was complete. The task was admittedly difficult, but missionaries were all too easily seen as agents of a foreign government whose policies brought death and destruction.

Fourthly, Elizabeth should have curbed the ability of the Irish nobles to defy the authority of the Crown. Any success here was compromised by the defiance of Tyrone, whose power in Ulster remained undimmed into the reign of the first Stuart king.

Lastly, what was the cost of Elizabethan rule to Ireland itself? By the time of Elizabeth's death, large areas of the country – particularly Ulster – had been devastated. Crops were burned, trade disrupted, and towns in ruins. Famine was widespread, and parts of the rich land of Munster were uninhabited. The prospect of an assimilation of such an Ireland within an English nation-state was remote indeed.

10 Scotland: An Introduction

Elizabeth's relations with Scotland almost entirely revolved around the figure of Mary Stuart, Queen of Scots. An account of the career of Mary reads like a particularly unlikely plot from a spectacularly extravagant and romantic historical novelist. Here we have a young Queen of Scotland: a woman, it seems, of beauty, intelligence and charm. She marries the young heir to the throne of France, and becomes Queen of France on his accession as Francis II. But Francis dies young, and the widow returns to her native Scottish shores. She already has a claim to the throne of England, and marries an English nobleman – Lord Darnley – who has a claim of his own. But the marriage is unhappy. The jealous Darnley snatches from his queen's presence a favourite of hers – the Italian secretary, David Riccio – and murders him in cold blood. However, Darnley is himself murdered. His house is blown up, and his strangled body is found in the garden. Suspicion falls on the Scottish nobleman, James Bothwell. Mary marries none other than Bothwell, and is imprisoned by horrified opponents. She subsequently escapes to England, where, after years of imprisonment, she is executed by the English Queen.

Although this sequence of events seems desperately improbable (a publisher with an eye for sensational fiction might be impressed), yet the basic factual outline is accurate. Most significant is Elizabeth's action. To execute a fellow monarch hardly seems in keeping with her general obsession with the rights of legitimate authority. The implication is, of course, that Mary represented a particularly dangerous threat to Elizabeth herself. The following two sections explain the nature of this threat, which lay partly in the uncertainties and tensions of traditional Anglo-Scottish relations and partly in the unique position of Mary herself.

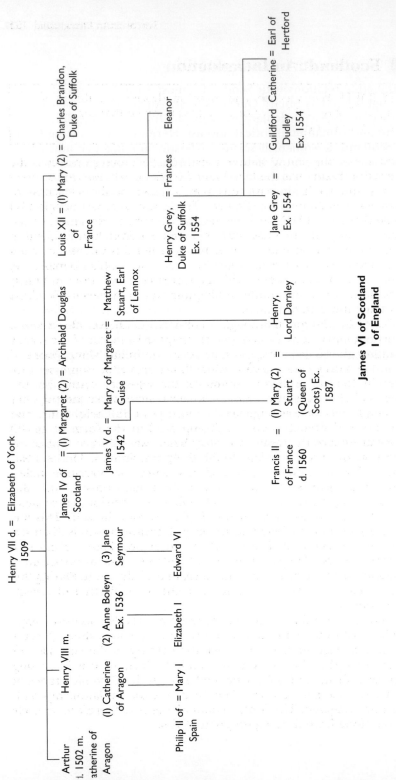

Family tree of the Tudor dynasty

11 The Scottish Background

> **KEY ISSUES** Why was Scotland traditionally seen as a threat by
> England? Why did Mary Stuart appear to make that threat
> significantly worse?

It was one of the central assumptions of English foreign policy in the
sixteenth century that the kingdom of Scotland represented a threat
to England. In large part, this was because of the closeness of
Scotland's relations with France. From the French perspective,
England was the traditional enemy. It therefore made sense for the
French to exploit the antagonism between Scotland and England to
damage the latter as much as possible. Chapter 5 contains a detailed
discussion of this issue (see page 92). From the Scottish perspective,
England was a real danger. With a far greater population and vastly
greater resources, the southern kingdom was an adversary Scotland
could not afford to face alone.

The earlier Tudors had sought to draw Scotland ever closer to the
English orbit. Henry VIII had, in fact, proposed a union of the realms
through a marriage of his son Edward to the infant Mary Queen of
Scots. Following Henry VIII's death, Lord Protector Somerset proposed in 1548 the self-same union on the self-same terms: but the
Scots saw behind the offer, not a mutually beneficial partnership, but
the simple loss of sovereignty to a more powerful neighbour. The
Scots invoked French help, which appeared in the form of 10,000
troops in June of the same year. Mary Stuart was taken to France for
education and then marriage to the Dauphin, Francis. This was bad
enough from the English point of view, since the marriage underpinned the Scottish–French alliance in the firmest possible way. But
the full danger was apparent on Elizabeth's accession, since Mary
Stuart had a strong claim to the English throne herself. This was
based largely on the alleged illegitimacy of Elizabeth, and is discussed
in detail in section 12. The French might exploit Mary's claim in a
number of ways. The powerful Guise family saw it as an opportunity
to destabilise the heretical Protestant regime of Elizabeth. Playing this
Catholic card was also a useful tactic in the bitter rivalries of French
court politics.

However, it would be a mistake to assume that all Scots were happy
to fall in with the world-view of the Guises. To some, their Queen's
foreign marriage seemed to reduce the country to the very state of
dependency they had striven to avoid. In fact, to the increasing
number of Protestant nobles, dependence on the Catholic France of
the Guises seemed a worse fate than a closer relationship with
Protestant England. The Scottish outlook was not, therefore, entirely
without hope from the English point of view.

12 Mary Stuart and the English Succession

> **KEY ISSUES** How strong a case could be made for Mary Stuart as the rightful queen (in place of Elizabeth) or as her successor? In what way did Mary Stuart shape the objectives of English policy towards Scotland?

The genealogical table on page 130 shows that, by hereditary descent, Mary Stuart was Elizabeth's rightful heir. The Scottish queen was a grandchild of Henry VIII's elder sister Margaret (wife of James IV of Scotland). On the same principle, next in line would be Margaret Douglas, Countess of Lennox, who was a daughter of Margaret Tudor's second marriage. Both Mary Stuart and Margaret Douglas would be welcomed by Catholics. On the other hand, the last will and testament of Henry VIII by-passed the Catholic heirs by granting the succession (assuming the death of Henry's own children without issue) to the children of his younger and Protestant sister Mary, Duchess of Suffolk. The representative of this line was, in Elizabeth's time, Lady Catherine Grey – a woman whose secret marriage had earned her both the enmity of Elizabeth and a ruling by the ecclesiastical courts that declared the marriage null and void. In any case, Henry VIII's will was a legal minefield. Firstly, its exact whereabouts was uncertain. It was also open to doubt whether the King had the right to alter traditional rules of inheritance. Admittedly, that right had been granted to the King by Parliament, but Parliament's right so to do was at least open to question. Also, setting aside the claims of Mary Stuart would be deemed unacceptable by traditionalists for whom laws of inheritance were sacred, irrespective of religious difference, political convenience or personal dislike.

To consider Mary as the rightful Queen in place of Elizabeth was another matter. There was no dispute that Elizabeth was the daughter of Henry VIII, but was she his rightful heir? After all, if one were to argue that her mother Anne Boleyn's marriage to the King was illegal – on the grounds that the King's previous marriage to Catherine of Aragon was never lawfully dissolved – then Elizabeth's title to the throne might be brought into question. In theory, English Catholics might take this line. After all, the dissolution of the Aragon marriage had been steadfastly opposed by the Pope. The dissolution had also, of course, led to Henry VIII's break with the Church of Rome. In practice, however, very few English Catholics disputed Elizabeth's title. Bitter enemies like the Guises had, needless to say, no such qualms. Mary's use of the royal arms of England was a sign of the antagonism that the Guises felt towards the English Queen, but no more than that. It should not be interpreted as the first step towards an intended invasion of England by France. Elizabeth was annoyed, but not alarmed, by Mary's behaviour.

Mary's claim to the succession, however, was another matter. It caused Elizabeth's councillors much additional anxiety. From the viewpoint of many Protestants in and outside the Privy Council, Mary's Catholicism rendered her unacceptable as Elizabeth's successor. This made it imperative in their eyes that Elizabeth should marry quickly to provide a Protestant heir. As Elizabeth grew older and hopes of her marriage began to fade, Mary's importance increased. The danger was that Elizabeth might lose the allegiance of those who kept their eyes fixed firmly on the future. Finally, there was the nightmare suffered by those convinced of the existence of an international Catholic conspiracy. Might not supporters of Mary wish to secure her succession by the simple expedient of murdering Elizabeth? As we shall see, fears for Elizabeth's safety grew as relations with Catholic Spain worsened.

Mary Stuart, then, was a convenient focus and weapon for all those who opposed the reign of Elizabeth I on religious grounds. In the following sections, we must trace the various challenges this posed to the government of Elizabeth and identify the policy of that government towards the Scottish Queen. In so doing, it should be possible to answer questions vital to any analysis of the nature and success of English policy. To what extent was the Queen responsible for Scottish policy? How far was policy clearly thought out? Did it merely respond to events, or was there evidence of long-term planning? What were the principles whereby relations with Mary were conducted? What changes, if any, were made to such principles?

13 Rebellion in Scotland, 1559

> **KEY ISSUES** How does support for the Lords of the Congregation and the resulting Treaty of Edinburgh reveal divisions between Elizabeth and Cecil?

In the spring of 1559, Protestant nobles – calling themselves Lords of the Congregation – rose in rebellion against the French Catholic regent of Scotland, Mary of Guise (mother of Mary Stuart). Their motives were partly religious, but also reflected their resentment at what they saw as a loss of Scottish sovereignty stemming from the links with France. This rebellion could be seen, of course, as a great opportunity for England. Support for the rebels, carefully emphasising a common Protestantism, might lead to a new relationship with Scotland which would go some way towards lessening the threat apparently posed by the Guises. In July 1559, Henry II of France died. The young French king and queen – Francis II and Mary Stuart – were encouraged by the Guise faction to use the coat of arms of the monarchs of England. Councillors such as William Cecil saw this as a clear confirmation of the existence of a Catholic plan to press the claims of Mary to the throne of England, while at the same time securing control of Scotland. They therefore pressed for immediate military intervention in Scotland.

What Cecil had to reckon with was Elizabeth's attitude towards the Scottish rebels. Elizabeth, as ever, showed little enthusiasm for international Protestant solidarity and had no intention of hiding her dislike of the religious mentor of the Lords of the Congregation, John Knox. Knox's pamphlet of 1558, *The First Blast of the Trumpet against the Monstrous Regiment of Women*, had been targeted at Mary of Guise and Mary I of England, but its savage criticism of women in positions of government had deeply offended Elizabeth. In addition, previous chapters have stressed Elizabeth's obsession with the rights of monarchs and the duties of subjects. To aid and abet rebels was wrong, and the fact that it was politically advantageous to do so did not, in Elizabeth's view, make it right. Elizabeth was, of course, also consulting her own personal interest. To encourage rebels in other countries might also encourage rebels at home. Elizabeth's attitude towards rebellion meant, on the one hand, that she was frequently unable to take advantage of situations as they arose – as a true pragmatist would have done – and, on the other, that she was dismissive of policies which genuinely sought to further the long-term interests of the nation itself. Fortunately for those interests, William Cecil was aware of the Queen's unwillingness to support the Lords of the Congregation. However, he managed to play upon her anger at the French royal couple's claim to her title to propel her into providing some grudging assistance for the rebels. Starting with the secret supply of arms and money to the Scots, she was then persuaded to send a fleet to the Firth of Forth to prevent any French attempt to relieve their main garrison in the town of Leith. Cecil also managed to get an English army sent to Scotland to assist with the siege of Leith in March 1560. The French agreed to negotiate in June, and the resulting Treaty of Edinburgh was something of a triumph for the English. The withdrawal of all English and French troops from Scotland was agreed upon, and the French commissioners promised that Mary Stuart would not use the royal arms of England. Mary herself refused to ratify the treaty, but this did not hinder the withdrawal of French troops.

It is important to note that credit must be given to William Cecil for the successful action resulting in the Treaty of Edinburgh. Elizabeth's part was performed with reluctance and a kind of brutal indecisiveness which drove her councillors to distraction. The Queen nearly managed to strangle the Edinburgh treaty at birth by sending last-minute instructions to Cecil in which he was told to refuse to sign unless the French agreed to hand over Calais and a substantial sum of money. Fortunately, she was too late. The treaty had already been signed.

It is doubtful whether the Queen was particularly happy with Cecil's achievement. Having encouraged subjects to rebel, her government had contributed greatly to the setting up of a Protestant regime in Scotland whose clerical leader – Knox – she detested. This, added to her parsimony, no doubt explains why she both refused to pay pensions to needy Scots lords who might be relied upon to support the anti-Guise government and also to reward those who had been instrumental in setting up the regime in the first place. England's political advantage was to play second fiddle to Elizabeth's assumptions on the rights of princes.

14 The Return of Mary Stuart

> **KEY ISSUE** Why was the Darnley marriage a significant blow to Elizabeth's interests?

Francis II died in December 1560. Mary Stuart's position in French politics collapsed along with that of the Guises as Catherine de Medici asserted her control (see page 94). Mary therefore returned to Scotland, where her presence raised many awkward questions for England. First and foremost was marriage. English councillors were all too aware that in Mary Stuart they had on their doorstep a young widow with a rich dowry. Since Mary was the unrecognised but legitimate heir to Elizabeth, this made the Queen of Scots's next marriage of vital interest to the security of England. Meanwhile, Elizabeth's apparent lack of interest in marrying was a source of enormous frustration to those Protestants for whom the prospect of a Catholic heir was too much to bear. Whatever were her reasons, it must be accepted that Elizabeth's failure to marry placed her personal feelings above the interests of her kingdom. After all, her elder sister and brother had died young, and, in 1562, she in her turn nearly succumbed to an attack of smallpox.

Back in her kingdom, Mary Stuart showed an astute grasp of political realities. On arrival, she had issued a proclamation forbidding any alteration in the state of religion as she found it. This meant an acceptance of the Protestant ascendancy. Mary never officially ratified Acts of 1560 which had condemned the Catholic Mass, but her administration did not seek to overturn them. Similarly, while she did insist on her right to practise her own faith, she was prepared to attend Protestant baptisms and weddings when it was politically expedient to do so. Her apparently statesmanlike behaviour and her genuine charm had secured the loyalty of important men who had no liking for her religion. One such example was William Maitland of Lethington. Secretary of State under Mary of Guise, he also held the post under Mary and showed himself to be an excellent advocate for her case to be officially recognised as Elizabeth's heir.

Mary's qualities could only be viewed with disquiet by her English Protestant opponents. Clearly, if Elizabeth could not be propelled into marriage, then it was vital to her interests that Mary be persuaded to marry a candidate acceptable to England. Ideally, this would be an English Protestant nobleman. The Scots felt – until enlightened – that Elizabeth had in mind Henry Darnley, son of the Countess of Lennox. But Darnley was anything but Elizabeth's candidate, since he had Catholic sympathies and, through his mother, something of a claim of his own to the English throne (see the genealogical table on page 130). Elizabeth, extraordinarily enough, proposed her favourite, Dudley, as Mary's suitor. The Scots assumed that this idea was a mere ploy to delay any marriage, and so was not to be treated seriously. This is very possible. But it is just conceivable that Elizabeth felt a Dudley marriage to be a sound move. She may have been sufficiently arrogant to believe that she could preside over a curious three-way relationship and groom her favourite's children to take over her throne.

In fact, Mary had little intention of accepting Elizabeth's promptings. She had hoped for a match with the son of the King of Spain, but was disappointed. She therefore turned to Darnley, and benefited from a miscalculation on the part of Elizabeth and Cecil. As an English subject, Darnley needed permission from Elizabeth to visit Scotland. The government raised no objection when Darnley made his request; presumably because it was felt that there was no prospect of such a match taking place. But, while he was in Scotland, Mary ennobled and then married Darnley in July 1565. The Protestant ascendancy in Scotland was shaken. Both Maitland and the Earl of Moray – half-brother of Mary Stuart – found their positions under threat and their advice suddenly unwelcome. Moray, after an abortive rebellion, fled to England.

How dangerous was the English miscalculation? Firstly, the Darnley marriage had been a grave blow to the ascendancy of the Protestant Scottish nobles with whom the Privy Council had established a sound working relationship. The Treaty of Edinburgh looked like so much waste paper. English Catholics would be encouraged by the prospect of co-religionists succeeding in time to the English throne. Admittedly, there was little immediate threat to Elizabeth. Whatever Mary Stuart might boast in unguarded moments, the Scots were too disunited and poor to constitute a military danger. But this was little real consolation to men such as Cecil whose antipathy to Mary Stuart and her religion led them to see the Darnley marriage as part of the alleged international Catholic plot against Europe's foremost Protestant power. There was, however, nothing much they could do about it. Attempts to provide major military backing for nobles such as Moray would be expensive: nor would the Queen sanction an attempt to depose Mary Stuart. It is therefore hard to avoid the conclusion that the early successes of English foreign policy in Scotland counted for little. Force of circumstance, some miscalculation and her antipathy towards marriage had left Elizabeth looking extremely vulnerable in the longer term. As the years went by, how was the Virgin Queen to keep the loyalty of nobles who could see that the future lay with the children of the Stuart and Lennox line? For, by January 1566, Mary was expecting a child.

15 Mary Stuart and the Murder of Darnley

> **KEY ISSUES**   What was Elizabeth's reaction to the deposition of Mary Stuart? In what way did the reaction of Elizabeth's councillors differ?

What jeopardised Mary Stuart's strong position in her relationship with Elizabeth was the unhappiness of her marriage to Darnley and the extraordinary and torrid series of events that resulted from it. In March 1566, Darnley and some of his friends dragged Mary's Italian secretary, David Riccio, from her presence and murdered him. Darnley's motive was jealousy and his action an indictment, not only of himself, but also of the Queen's indiscreet conduct. There were no dramatic repercussions immediately. Perhaps profiting from the antagonism between Darnley and Mary, Moray returned to Scotland and was reconciled with his half-sister. Meanwhile, Mary's envoy, Sir James Melville, travelled to England in the hope that Elizabeth might be persuaded into a formal acceptance of Mary and her new-born son, James, as her successors. This he was unable to achieve, but it seems clear that a number of very influential nobles were keen to reveal themselves privately to be in favour of his suit. These included Norfolk – the most powerful nobleman in the country – and, oddly enough, Leicester himself. The latter's motives may well have been an understandable desire to safeguard himself once his status as favourite was no longer any protection.

Then, in February 1567, came the murder of Darnley. Mary's complicity was apparently all too clear when she married the Earl of Bothwell, the very man suspected of being responsible for her husband's death. Mary's exact state of mind at this time can only be guessed at. The fact that she was prepared to marry Bothwell according to Protestant rites is significant: for whatever reason, emotion had overpowered her shrewd political sense. The ensuing turmoil gave an opportunity for Moray to lead a Protestant faction which seized the Queen, forced her to abdicate and crowned her child as James VI. Moray was regent, but his position was weak when he was confronted by those who could not stomach an unprecedented and forced abdication, however much they might wish for the downfall of Bothwell.

Elizabeth was, unsurprisingly, aghast at the deposition, and sent an envoy to demand the release and restoration of the former Queen of Scots. Indeed, Elizabeth was in a state bordering on frenzy. It does not seem to have occurred to her that an unhoped-for opportunity existed to rebuild a pro-English regime in Scotland. What mattered to her was not political expediency, but the political principle nearest to her heart – the inalienable rights of the legitimate ruler. Even when Mary fled to England in the summer of 1568, Elizabeth persisted in considering how she could restore her. However, her councillors persuaded her to postpone any action, suggesting that Mary might be subject to some kind of judicial investigation into her role in the death of Darnley. This would at least give the government some breathing space in which to decide what to do with her.

16 Mary in England

> **KEY ISSUES** (to cover sections 16–18) Why, in the face of Catholic plots, was Elizabeth so reluctant to heed her councillors' calls for Mary's execution? What were the circumstances of that execution?

Mary in England posed particular problems – even in her place of custody in 'remote' Staffordshire. Her behaviour in Scotland had not affected her claim to the succession to the throne of England, and her actual presence in England might well loosen the allegiance of Catholics to Elizabeth. It was also conceivable that she would be the centre of plots to assassinate Elizabeth. After all, assassination on religious grounds was not uncommon in contemporary Europe. In addition, even Mary's implacable opponent Cecil was aware that she had considerable political skill and personal magnetism. These qualities and the passing of time would efface the charges that were laid against her by Moray in front of the Privy Council. Certainly Mary could not be allowed the freedom – at the English court or elsewhere – to build up a faction to support her claims.

It seemed, however, that Mary did not need personal liberty to attract support. By the spring of 1569, it would seem that some people of great influence were prepared to recognise Mary's position as Elizabeth's heir, providing she were safely married to a suitable Englishman. The premier nobleman of England – the Duke of Norfolk – was the most obvious candidate. However, he was not unsympathetic to Catholicism. It is a sign of the dangers posed by Elizabeth's continued avoidance of marriage that a group in support of the Norfolk marriage included Leicester. Were the marriage to take place, then the way might then be open for the restoration of Mary to her Scottish throne.

It was only a question of time before Elizabeth heard of the scheme. Leicester, making the best of it he could, tearfully confessed and retired to the comparative safety of his sick-bed. Norfolk was summoned to court and informed in no uncertain terms that he was to give up any such plans. However, the situation was more volatile than Elizabeth realised. Norfolk was faced with Mary's demands that he should release her by force if necessary. At the same time he was under pressure from certain northern earls to mobilise his supporters to free Mary, go through with the marriage and place pressure on Elizabeth to recognise Mary as her successor. It is clear that some sort of rising in the north had been planned. The northern earls – Northumberland and Westmorland – were Catholic themselves and had estates in the counties of the north least affected by Protestantism. But once Norfolk, after some agonised consultation with his own followers, had submitted to Elizabeth and was lodged in the Tower of London, Northumberland and Westmorland found themselves out on a limb. They were themselves summoned to the royal presence, but were too compromised by their discussion of the succession and contacts with the Pope and Spain to risk their fates at court. They were therefore pushed into open rebellion.

17 The Revolt of the Northern Earls and the Ridolfi Plot

Pages 67–8 contain a discussion of the course and failure of the rebellion. The Duke of Norfolk had survived despite his links with the rebels, but had learned little from his narrow escape. He would not give up the prospect of marriage with Mary: a testimony to the influence of her presence on Catholic sympathisers. Mary, quite naturally, was more than ready to pursue any channel which would free her from her irksome captivity. She became embroiled in the schemings of one Roberto di Ridolfi, an Italian merchant with connections in many European courts. Ridolfi had a plan for seeking military assistance for Mary from the Spanish commander in the Netherlands, the Duke of Alva. Norfolk was persuaded by Ridolfi to agree to a request for such assistance. Were that to be forthcoming, Norfolk was to raise his own followers. The plot was discovered, and Norfolk's role exposed. At his trial in January 1572, his defence largely consisted of the argument that he was a duke, and therefore that his word counted for far more than anyone else's. This was not well received. Norfolk was duly executed in June 1572.

Mary Stuart was herself in some danger. Cecil – now Lord Burghley – was instrumental in leading the Privy Council to put pressure on the Queen to have Mary executed. The Parliament of 1572 was probably called due to unremitting pressure from the privy councillors, who hoped that acts would be passed to attaint the Queen of Scots and to exclude her from the succession. Elizabeth fought these proposals with her customary skill. She refused to have anything to do with the Attainder Bill, and diverted Parliament's attention to the Exclusion Bill, which she then shelved.

The massacre of the French Protestants on St Bartholomew's Day (August 1572) simply confirmed the views of those who, like Burghley, assumed the existence of a murderous Catholic conspiracy – a conspiracy represented in England, of course, by Mary Stuart. Elizabeth remained, as ever, unmoved by the renewed pleas to put Mary to death. It may be that she had now discarded any real intention of restoring Mary to her Scottish throne, but the gulf between Elizabeth's attitude to Mary and that of her Privy Council was nevertheless distressingly wide. This meant that genuine discussion and calm planning on this issue became impossible. The councillors therefore had to find other ways to influence the Queen: and the best method was to frighten her with details of immediate and personal threats to herself and her throne.

18 The Downfall of Mary Stuart

The political climate of the 1580s provided just such an opportunity. In 1580, a papal pronouncement stated that anyone who assassinated Elizabeth with the 'pious intention of doing God service not only does not sin, but gains merit'. In 1584, the murder of William of Orange provided apparent evidence that all Protestant monarchs were in danger from Catholic terrorism. The same year saw the exposure of the Throckmorton Plot in England, in which the Duke of Guise was to lead an invasion aimed at releasing Mary Stuart and deposing Elizabeth. Burghley and Walsingham were sufficiently alarmed to draw up the Bond of Association (October 1584), by which signatories pledged to defend Elizabeth by force and, in effect, to murder anyone implicated in plots against the monarch. The Bond was never invoked as such, but the highly-charged atmosphere, in which fear of Jesuit missionaries coincided with fear of Spanish invasion, had its effect on Elizabeth herself. She was frightened, and a frightened Elizabeth was an insecure safeguard for Mary Stuart.

Concern over the threat of Spain led Elizabeth and her councillors to act together in seeking a defensive league with James VI against Spain. James, after all, had little to gain from a Spanish invasion of England. Only his mother stood between him and the succession to the throne of England after Elizabeth's death. He did, however, stand to gain a useful pension if he accepted such a league. In 1585, the league was formalised and James received an annual pension of about £4000. Informally, this meant that he was accepting his mother's continued imprisonment. The policy of keeping James reasonably happy with the pension and subsidies was sensible, although few councillors trusted him. What was even more attractive to the young king than money was a letter written by Elizabeth which promised that nothing should be done to harm his title to the English Crown.

For Mary, a Spanish invasion was her last hope of freedom and, just possibly, of the prize that had never been close enough for her to grasp – the throne of England. In May 1586, she formally disinherited her son in favour of the King of Spain in the hope that this would stimulate Spanish efforts on her behalf. In this way, the seeds for her eventual execution were sown, as she could not resist dabbling in further plots against Elizabeth. In 1586, Anthony Babington, a fervent Catholic and supporter of Jesuit missions, was in contact by letter with Mary. His offer was straightforward enough: to release Mary and subsequently murder Elizabeth. Mary appears to have dictated a letter in reply which endorsed the plan, with the suggestion that Elizabeth should be murdered before, rather than after, Mary's release. But matters of timing were all irrelevant, because the whole correspondence was being read with much satisfaction by Walsingham himself. Babington was arrested, and readily confessed his part in the whole scheme. But what was to happen to Mary herself? A committee of nobles, privy councillors and justices meeting at Mary's new place of custody, Fotheringay Castle, found her guilty of plotting to assassinate Elizabeth. Elizabeth refused to have the sentence published, and the Privy Council persuaded her to summon Parliament in the hope that she could be forced by sheer weight of opinion to sign a death warrant. Parliament duly petitioned for Mary's execution. Even so, the Queen would not commit herself. Her chronic indecision was fed by her simple revulsion at condemning to death a fellow monarch and a fear of the likely reactions of neighbouring states – particularly, of course, the King of Scotland. It is a mark of Elizabeth's desperation that she should, against advice, sound out Mary's Puritan gaoler, Sir Amyas Paulet, on the possibility of his disposing of Mary without implicating the Queen. Not unreasonably, Paulet refused. His letter to the Queen took the high moral ground. His life was, he said, in Elizabeth's hands:

> ... but God forbid that I should make so foul a shipwreck of my conscience or leave so great a blot to my poor posterity to shed blood without law or warrant.

The warrant, indeed, was all ready for signature: but how was the Queen to be persuaded to sign it? Once again, the Privy Council tried to force Elizabeth to act by playing on her fears for her own safety. She was fed fictitious stories about Spanish landings in Wales and Mary's escape. Pen and ink were sent for, and she signed the warrant, but instructed her second secretary, Davison, not to have it sealed and dispatched. Davison, however, sealed it and dashed off to consult his fellow councillors. The decision was taken to dispatch the warrant and not to tell the Queen until the execution was over. Mary was beheaded on 8 February 1587, and the Queen turned – with all appearance of genuine fury – on Davison. He found himself heavily fined and a prisoner in the Tower of London. Burghley was denied access to the Queen for a month. In the meantime, Elizabeth wrote letters to James VI in which she proclaimed her innocence. James was only too pleased to receive such protestations. They enabled him to avoid a military conflict with a country whose crown he was now closer to gaining than ever before.

19 Mary Queen of Scots: A Summary

> **KEY ISSUES** How successful was English policy towards Scotland? To what can success be attributed?

It could be argued that, following Mary's execution, the central aims of English policy towards Scotland had been achieved. Mary's death was a particularly clear fulfilment of the aim to neutralise her influence. The Scottish king was reasonably friendly towards a kingdom he fully expected to inherit, and the possibility of the French or Spanish using Scotland as a weapon against England was non-existent. On the other hand, it is hard to escape the conclusion that good fortune played the major role in an eminently satisfactory outcome. Indeed, if attention is turned to the actions of the English government, we see frequent turmoil, miscalculation and delay – all fuelled by Elizabeth's parsimony, prejudice and indecisiveness and by disagreements with councillors on priorities.

It is impossible to assess the extent to which Elizabeth was in actual danger of assassination because of Mary's presence and willingness to engage in plots. But it is fair to say that the danger would have been less if Mary were not so near at hand and so convenient a rallying-point and incentive for Catholic extremists. Of course, had Elizabeth married and borne children, then the danger of Mary Stuart would have been largely neutralised. Only a few Catholic die-hards would have remembered a one-time Scottish queen residing in comfortable prisons in the midlands of England. Those prepared to murder Elizabeth might have baulked at the thought of murdering a royal family.

Speculation apart, how effectively was Mary Stuart handled as Elizabeth's prisoner? Certainly, the Privy Council responded efficiently to the need to keep her secure. There was little or no prospect of even her most enthusiastic and imaginative rescuers freeing her. The surveillance system established by Walsingham produced the evidence needed to convict her. As for Elizabeth herself, her refusal to be steam-rollered by her Privy Council and Parliament into executing Mary – particularly after the Ridolfi Plot – made sound political sense. The effect of an execution at that time on the fraught relations with Spain and France could hardly have been positive. On the other hand, Elizabeth's refusal probably owed more to her beliefs in the inviolability of the monarch's position than to political acumen. In the event, the manner of Mary's execution gave James VI the opportunity to avoid a military confrontation with England: but again, this owed more to the fortunate combination of Elizabeth's dithering and a convenient scapegoat than it did to political expertise.

20 The Final Years: Relations with James VI

Elizabeth's failure to marry has been seen as a symptom of her lack of interest in the fate of her country after her death. This monumental egotism also informed her relationship with her most likely successor, the King of Scotland. James was never officially promised the succession, and it is unlikely that Elizabeth bothered to name him on her deathbed. James succeeded because he was the only realistic candidate, and was supported at the centre of English government by men such as Burghley's son, Robert Cecil. When Elizabeth died on 24 March 1603, they were in the position to issue a proclamation announcing James's accession. It was a curious end to the Tudors' relationship with Scotland. Henry VIII had wanted to assimilate Scotland into England: his second daughter had shown no such interest. The line of the Tudor monarchs died out as the King of Scotland took the English throne.

Summary Diagram
Elizabeth and Ireland

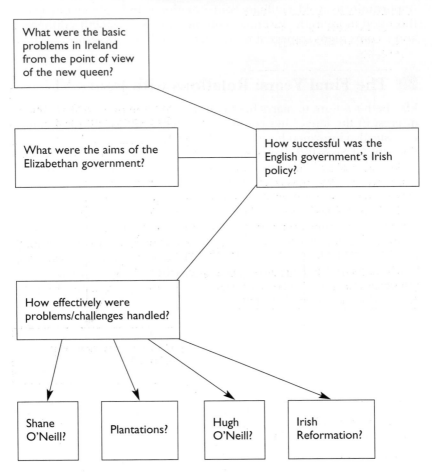

Summary Diagram
Elizabeth and Scotland

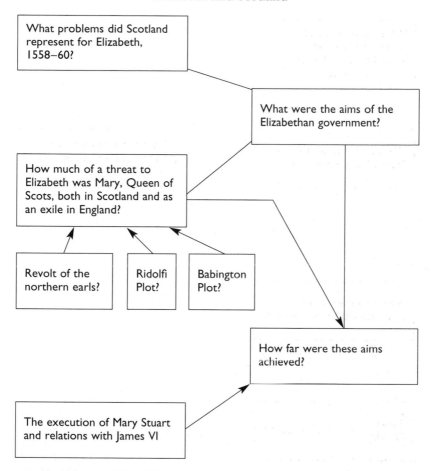

What problems did Scotland represent for Elizabeth, 1558–60?

What were the aims of the Elizabethan government?

How much of a threat to Elizabeth was Mary, Queen of Scots, both in Scotland and as an exile in England?

Revolt of the northern earls?

Ridolfi Plot?

Babington Plot?

How far were these aims achieved?

The execution of Mary Stuart and relations with James VI

Working on Chapter 6

Your note-making should follow the basic division of the chapter, where Ireland and Scotland are treated separately. Note-making needs a sense of direction, so you should target the following issues: what were the aims of Elizabeth and her councillors? (remembering to distinguish between the different aims).
What specific problems did Elizabeth face?
How successfully were those aims achieved?

The best approach would be in table form, using columns headed
AIMS
PROBLEMS
SUCCESS

Answering structured and essay questions on Chapter 6

Essay questions relevant to Chapter 6 are usually reasonably straight-forward. First of all, it is unlikely – although not, of course, impossible – that you would be asked to cover both Ireland and Scotland in one essay.

Most questions require an assessment of Elizabeth's performance in dealing with Ireland *or* Scotland. The standard method of structuring this kind of essay is to discuss what Elizabeth's aims were, what problems she faced and to assess achievement accordingly.

Questions appear quite frequently which are focused entirely on Mary, Queen of Scots. These generally involve an analysis of the extent to which she was a threat to Elizabeth. Beware, however, of assuming that a question on Elizabeth's relations with Scotland requires nothing more than a discussion of Mary Stuart.

It is possible that a more wide-ranging question would step beyond the boundaries of this chapter – or even of this book. 'How effectively did the Tudors cope with the problem of Scotland?' is, of course, beyond the scope of *Elizabeth I: Religion and Foreign Affairs*. Questions like 'How far was English Catholicism a threat to Elizabeth I?' are not, but require an awareness of how Mary Stuart fits into the context of the 'Catholic problem'. This issue is discussed mainly in Chapter 4.

Also possible is the question linking Scotland and France. Here is one example: 'Elizabeth's policy towards Scotland and France was more pragmatic than principled." Comment on this view.' To answer this question properly, you will need to have studied Chapter 5 in addition to this chapter. But a few general points need to be made at this stage. As has been argued in previous guidance sections, when dealing with questions asking you to comment on a statement, it is absolutely vital that you establish from the very beginning what your view is. The essay should therefore be structured around your argument. You may feel, for example, that the statement in the above question, while not without truth, is seriously flawed. Is it not the case that Elizabeth maintained certain basic principles – such as the unwillingness to help rebels – which were then buffeted by circumstance? 'Pragmatic' is therefore inaccurate. This kind of statement of your argument leads you into the development of your essay and reminds you of the need to make the information supplied relevant to your view. It may also help you to avoid mistakes in structure. The temptation in the essay above is to attempt to treat Scotland and France entirely separately. This would probably lead to confusion, since, as we know, policy towards France frequently had important implications for Scotland and *vice versa*.

7 Conclusion

1 Writing Conclusions

Few students like writing conclusions to essays. Often advised to 'sum up' their arguments, they feel that they can offer little more than a bare repetition prefaced by the phrase 'in conclusion'. The present writer has much sympathy with this predicament. Writing a conclusion to this book has its own difficulties! After all, a bare summary of the conclusions of the various chapters would be 'old hat' and of little value to students who are unlikely to be asked examination questions covering all aspects of religious policy and foreign affairs.

Arguably, the best conclusions should provide a terse and vivid picture of the main lines of argument. They should also seek to place the discussions in a wider context. One of the great attractions and dangers of history is that we seem to know what happened next, and it is therefore important to explore – albeit briefly – the impact made by your subject on its own future. It is also fair and scholarly to admit to the limitations of your conclusions and to point out, if possible, where further investigation should be targeted. Hopefully, this concluding chapter will meet these aims.

2 Elizabeth and Religion

It is difficult to imagine Elizabeth forgetting – even for a moment – that she was Queen of England. Her rank was her obsession, and she played the part of Virgin Queen and nursing mother to her country with skill. But she was never the prisoner of her image. Her concept of queenship was narrow, and had more to do with maintaining her authority in a male-dominated world than with grandiose images of Old Testament prophetesses and the succouring of Protestantism. Religion was, therefore, a vital tool whereby she engineered her survival and safeguarded her position. In her own terms, Elizabeth's religious policy was a success. She felt it to be in her interest to establish a broadly-based national Church which excluded as few as possible. It was in her interest to make conformity to her religious settlement as easy as possible without encouraging disagreement within the Church of England or recusancy without. It has been argued in this book that the religious settlement as outlined in the Acts of Supremacy and Uniformity reflected the wishes of the Queen. The Church of England was, therefore, a Protestant Church with a Catholic hierarchical structure. Calvinist in theology, its rituals were at least similar to Catholicism. Those who sought to make the Church more Protestant were, in the Queen's eyes, dangerous subversives. At the very least, such moves would stimulate recusancy and, as a direct result, disobedience. At the worst, an England full of Protestant evangelists and godly, disciplined congregations would compromise the power of the bishops. And bishops were the mechanisms whereby the Queen maintained her control of the Church.

So the Queen succeeded in thwarting attempts to modify the settlement of 1559. By the end of her reign, Catholicism was on the way to becoming a religion of a minority of the gentry: its hold on the lower classes was waning and it was increasingly restricted to the areas of the country remote from London. From Elizabeth's point of view, this stifling of Catholicism was a considerable achievement and rendered more impressive when one takes into account the apparent weakness of Protestantism at the start of the reign. Not that it is easy to estimate the strength of popular religious belief. This explains, no doubt, why the issue is subject to intense historiographical debate.

There was a price to pay for Elizabeth's success, and whether the price was worthwhile depends largely on the attitude of the historian. It could be argued that Elizabeth missed an opportunity to utilise the enthusiasm of Puritans to create an aggressive and dynamic Church of England. She assumed that they represented a threat to her authority and silenced them. But would an aggressive and dynamic Church of England have been a good thing? Any answer to this question would perhaps rest more on the historian's religious preferences than on purely historical judgement. What is clear is that Elizabeth rarely hesitated to exploit the financial position of the Church in her own interests. This can only have weakened the very people chosen to impose her own concept of a Church upon the people: the bishops themselves.

Those historians who argue that Elizabeth's religious policy was liberal and far-sighted are in error on two counts. Firstly, it is anachronistic to call a sixteenth-century monarch 'liberal'. Secondly, the Queen had no interest in England after Elizabeth. Historians, however, *are* interested, and are aware that the Church as shaped by the Queen had a colossal impact on the religious and social life of the country – and beyond – through to the present day. The Thirtynine Articles, for instance, remain the central theological statement of the modern Church of England. But Elizabeth's religious legacy was not an easy one for her successors to handle. Since the compromises at the heart of the Elizabethan Church were inspired by political need, it required a shrewd politician to make a positive use of them. The Church of England was not a fully unified church, and there remained Roman Catholics and Protestant Separatists well and truly outside it. Diversity might, in the right hands, lead to genuine toleration; in the wrong hands, it might lead to division and strife. Charles I ably demonstrated what chaos the wrong hands could cause.

3 Elizabeth and Foreign Affairs

To remain Queen of England and to maintain her authority, to see that authority restricted by no foreign power and usurped by no councillor or recognised heir – these considerations lay at the heart of Elizabeth's conduct of foreign affairs. This interpretation has the advantage of complementing our picture of Elizabeth as Supreme Governor of the Church of England. It also accounts for the successes and limitations of her foreign policies.

It has been argued in this book that Elizabeth was captivated by none of the enthusiasms and grandiose visions of her Protestant councillors. She was not seduced by images of herself as the saviour of Protestantism. She assisted foreign rebels against Catholic overlords with obvious reluctance. The rebels of the Netherlands were not Protestant heroes and martyrs in her eyes, but rather distasteful and expensive subversives seeking to overthrow legitimate rulers. They were to be helped only when the security of Elizabeth's crown seemed threatened by French or Spanish dominance of the region. The major shifts in foreign policy, such as the increasing antagonism towards Spain and the increasing friendship towards France, came about because the former was replacing the latter as the major threat.

It could be argued that Elizabeth was the supreme realist and pragmatist who avoided shackling her second-rate (in terms of military power) country to risky and ruinous ventures abroad. It was certainly fortunate that Elizabeth was able to curb her aggressive councillors, but it is likely that indecision and parsimony had more to do with her actions than an admirable grasp of politics. It was never good policy to leave military commanders uncertain of the Queen's support, whether they were fighting in the Netherlands or in Ireland. It was never good policy to make a decision and then fail to back it up with sufficient funds. It was never good policy to appoint a man like Leicester to military commands.

Perhaps it is a lesson of sixteenth-century history that fortune favoured the indecisive. Philip II of Spain had his own problems in making major decisions, and when he did so disaster was all too frequently the result. The failure of his great Armada is a case in point. Elizabeth was certainly indecisive, and fortunate that the Armadas failed; fortunate that the opposition of the Guises faltered in the increasing turmoil of the French wars of religion; and doubly fortunate in the spectacular mistakes of her greatest rival, Mary Stuart.

By her own criteria, Elizabeth's foreign policy was a success. She had repelled threats to her crown from, at various times, France, Spain, Scotland and Ireland. She had ridden out the storms of religious division. Unlike France, her realm had not exhausted itself in civil war between Catholic and Protestant. Her refusal to marry and to name a successor had preserved her own authority. She had never sought to extend that authority through the vainglory of military conquest in the manner of her father. No doubt she shared Henry VIII's view that England was more a personal possession by right of inheritance than a sacred trust. But her propaganda for the home market, together with the religious upheavals in Europe, gave credence to the view that monarchs should actively seek, through their foreign policy, the good of the country. Her Stuart successors would have found it difficult to launch campaigns in Europe for reasons of personal prestige or dynastic advancement. It was just as well that James I was frightened by war.

4 Elizabeth and Marriage

A reminder of the tortuous and ultimately abortive marriage negotiations will help illustrate the way in which foreign affairs, religion and personalities intermingled. Susan Doran's judicious discussion of the courtships of Elizabeth[1] suggests that one should not look for an explanation for the failures of marriage negotiations in Elizabeth's psyche, but in the interplay of religious conviction and self-interest (both political and personal) amongst her councillors – an interplay which might both manipulate and be manipulated by Elizabeth herself.

The Queen appears to have genuinely wanted to marry on two occasions. Robert Dudley's candidature had the advantage of the Queen's favour but the even more telling disadvantage of the over-convenient and duly suspicious death of his wife and the antagonism of fellow councillors, who saw him as a factional opponent with several axes to grind. Francis of Anjou was again favoured by the Queen, but opposition within the council centred upon his insistence that, although he would forego public worship, he must be allowed to hear Mass privately. Some councillors saw this as an acceptable compromise. Some argued that one could not compromise with a pagan or devilish rite. Some felt that even a private Mass would encourage Catholic resistance. And Robert Dudley, aware that his intimacy with the Queen would not survive her marriage, was adept at exploiting such divisions. The Queen could, of course, similarly play the religious card when a proposed marriage – such as that with Archduke Charles – was less to her taste. In short, it seems likely that the Queen did not marry because there was never an occasion where both she and the overwhelming majority of her councillors were united in favour of any candidate. The marriage issue, then, is a useful snap-shot of the extent and limitations of the Queen's personal power as well as an example of the complex brew of religion, politics and personal interest which formed the high politics of the reign of Elizabeth I.

5 A Remarkable Woman

This heading was used in the introduction to this book. Its repetition is intended to remind readers of the stature of Elizabeth as a queen.

The present writer has had cause to criticise her policy-making on many occasions, but it is difficult – and perhaps inadvisable – to ignore the power of the Elizabethan cult over the Queen's own subjects and over most historians since. It is easy enough to point out how the ageing Queen insisted on her portraits appearing youthful and undimmed by time. Christopher Haigh charts effectively the slide in Elizabeth's popularity in the last years of her reign. But experience of James I soon ensured a revival in the adoration of Elizabeth I. This vision of the golden days of the Virgin Queen lacked a firm basis in reality, but it remains as a testimony to her qualities. Haigh points out that it was a remarkable achievement for a female ruler to survive at all. True enough: and all the more so because of the momentous problems Elizabeth faced for so long.

Reference

1 S. Doran, *Monarchy and Matrimony: the Courtships of Elizabeth I* (London, 1996)

Working on Chapter 7

This is not a chapter on which to make notes. It was suggested that conclusions should offer a vivid summary of the main interpretations, point out where further research needs to be done and, if necessary, place the themes studied in a wider context. It therefore makes sense to suggest that you should use this chapter as a quarry for your own conclusions to essays on Elizabeth, religion and foreign affairs.

Further Reading

1 Surveys

To help put Elizabeth, religion and foreign affairs into a wider context, the best modern survey is **John Guy**, *Tudor England* (OUP 1990). If your course is to include work on the Stuarts, the best survey is **Robert Ashton**, *Reformation and Revolution* (Paladin 1985).

2 Biographies

It is not possible to recommend a traditional-style biography of Elizabeth, since the vast majority tend to be rather uncritical, romantic and nationalist. One work which is less a biography than a cool and clear thematic analysis of Elizabeth's exercise of power is **Christopher Haigh**, *Elizabeth I* (Longman, second edition 1998). It would be useful to supplement the above with another volume under Haigh's editorship: **Christopher Haigh** (ed), *The Reign of Elizabeth I* (Macmillan 1984). The essays by **Jones**, **Ramsay**, **Collinson** and **Haigh** himself are well worth perusal.

3 Specialist Studies

There is no shortage of stimulating books on Elizabeth and religion. The debate between Dickens and the revisionists can be followed up in works by Haigh and Dickens: **Christopher Haigh**, *The English Reformation Revised* (CUP 1987) and *English Reformations* (Oxford 1993), **A.G. Dickens**, *The English Reformation* (OUP 1989). Make sure you get hold of this second edition of Dickens. For those who are interested in the development of the historiography of the English Reformation, a first-class work is **Rosemary O'Day**, *The Debate on the English Reformation* (Methuen 1986). This can be supplemented by **Susan Doran**'s brief Lancaster Pamphlet *Elizabeth I and Religion* (Routledge 1994), which offers a useful evaluation of Haigh's theses. The final chapter, which assesses the strengths and weaknesses of the Elizabethan church, is a helpful summary.

For Elizabeth and the Puritans, a challenging work is **Diarmaid MacCulloch**, *The Later Reformation in England* (Macmillan 1990). Full of fascinating detail is **Patrick Collinson**, *The Elizabethan Puritan Movement* (Cape 1967). This work succeeds in communicating the spirit of Puritanism. It is, however, very long. A more accessible text is **Patrick McGrath**, *Papists and Puritans Under Elizabeth I* (Blandford 1967). Although some of the interpretations are looking rather dated, the narrative remains very valuable.

For Elizabeth and the Catholics, see **Christopher Haigh**'s chapter

'The Church of England, the Catholics and the People' in *The Reign of Elizabeth I* and the chapter 'The Continuity of Catholicism in the English Reformation' by the same author in his *The English Reformation Revised*, both mentioned above. A good brief survey is **Alan Dures**, *English Catholicism, 1558–1642* (Longman 1983). For those interested in a Catholic perspective on the impact of the Elizabethan Reformation, the final chapter of **Eamon Duffy**'s *The Stripping of the Altars* (Yale 1992) is essential, but not easy.

Elizabethan foreign policy is perhaps less well served. An effective survey is **Susan Doran**, *England and Europe 1485–1603* (Longman 1986). This work is necessarily brief on the reign of Elizabeth, but the same author's Lancaster pamphlet *Elizabeth I and Foreign Policy* (Routledge 2000) offers an up-to-date discussion of the latest research. There is the **Ramsay** chapter in *The Reign of Elizabeth I* referred to above, but it also very brief. There are a number of volumes by **R.B. Wernham** which go to the opposite extreme and are, perhaps, far too lengthy for most A Level or undergraduate students unless they have a particular need for very considerable detail. If so, the most useful is **R.B. Wernham**, *After the Armada: Elizabethan England and the Struggle for Western Europe* (Oxford 1984). In similar detail are **Wallace T. MacCaffrey**, *The Shaping of the Elizabethan Regime* (London 1969), *Queen Elizabeth and the Making of Policy 1572–1588* (New Jersey 1981) and *Elizabeth I: War and Politics 1588–1603* (New Jersey 1992). **MacCaffrey**'s *Elizabeth I* (Arnold 1993) is best seen as an effective summary of the other books and is correspondingly more accessible.

Suitable works on Elizabeth and Scotland are very limited. For those of you who become fascinated by Mary Stuart, a work which charts various interpretations and provides a lucid commentary is **Ian Cowan**, *The Enigma of Mary Stuart* (Gollancz 1971). The author points to the difficulties of writing, and the dangers of reading, the meaty biographies of that fascinating but elusive Queen.

On Ireland, a work with a useful document section is **Grenfell Morton**, *Elizabethan Ireland* (Longman 1971). However, it is not easy to obtain. A complex and rewarding book for those who wish to study the subject in depth is **Steven Ellis**, *Tudor Ireland* (Longman 1985). **Mark Nicholls**' *A History of the Modern British Isles: The Two Kingdoms* (Oxford 1999) is also well worth consulting on both Ireland and Scotland.

Index